Northu... Coast Path

Roland Tarr, modern linguist and outdoors enthusiast, has served as Assistant Countryside Officer in Cheshire, Heritage Coast Officer in Dorset and has worked as a consultant in informal countryside recreation. He has always used photography to promote conservation and countryside recreation causes. He has close family connections to the north-east and has spent many happy days wandering the Northumbrian coast for over 50 years.

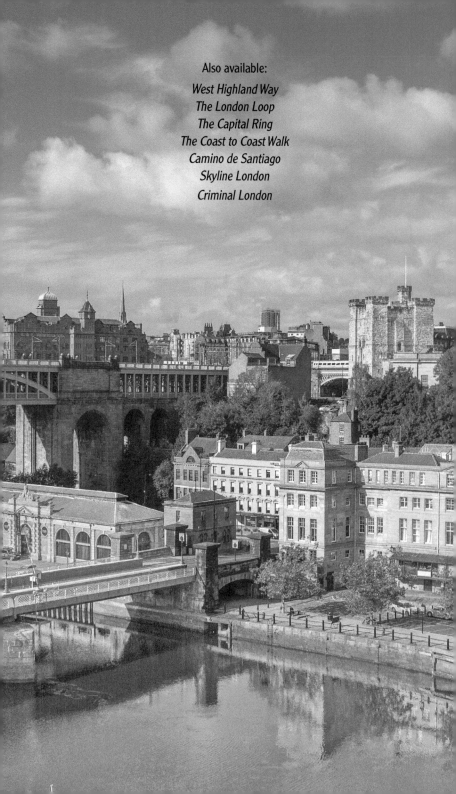

Also available:

West Highland Way
The London Loop
The Capital Ring
The Coast to Coast Walk
Camino de Santiago
Skyline London
Criminal London

Northumberland Coast Path

From the centre of Newcastle to the Scottish border

Text and photographs
Roland Tarr

Aurum
Press

Brimming with creative inspiration, how-to projects, and useful information to enrich your everyday life, Quarto Knows is a favourite destination for those pursuing their interests and passions. Visit our site and dig deeper with our books into your area of interest: Quarto Creates, Quarto Cooks, Quarto Homes, Quarto Lives, Quarto Drives, Quarto Explores, Quarto Gifts, or Quarto Kids.

Inspiring | Educating | Creating | Entertaining

Acknowledgements

My thanks to Dr Simon Conway Morris for the article on the geology of the Northumberland Coast, Ajay Tegala for checking Chapters 7 and 10 and Chris Rose for general advice on the birds.

This new edition published 2016 by Aurum Press
an imprint of the Quarto Group
The Old Brewery, 6 Blundell Street
London N7 9BH, United Kingdom
www.QuartoKnows.com

© 2013, 2016 Quarto Publishing plc
Text © 2013 Roland Tarr

All images by Roland Tarr, with the exception of the following:
25 NSCR; 26-27 © Ange/Alamy; 34 Tyne & Wear Archives & Museums;
96 © Alistair Laming/Alamy; 144 reproduced with permission of Northumberland Archives, 149 © Graeme Peacock/Alamy; 154 Clearview/Alamy.

A catalogue record for this book is available from the British Library.

ISBN 978 1 78131 562 0

Book designed by Carrdesignstudio • Printed and bound in the UK
Cover photograph: *Bamburgh Castle.*

MIX
Paper from responsible sources
FSC   FSC® C013604
www.fsc.org

Aurum Press want to ensure that these trail guides are always as up to date as possible – but stiles collapse, pubs close and bus services change all the time. If, on walking this path, you discover any important changes that future walkers need to be aware of, do let us know. Either send us an email to trailguides@quarto.com or, if you take the trouble to drop us a line to: **Trail Guides, Aurum Press, 74–77 White Lion Street, London N1 9PF,** we'll send you a free guide of your choice as thanks.

Contents

Transport • Tourist information centres • Accommodation • Useful websites •
Useful addresses • Smartphone and tablet maps • Other places to visit near
the Northumberland and Berwickshire coasts • Bibliography

How to use this guide

This guide to the Northumberland and Berwickshire coast paths, covering 134 miles (220 km) of the tidal coast of ancient Northumbria and the former Berwickshire, is in three parts.

• The introduction, which explains why you might want to walk this path, describes the sort of path it is, and gives some general information about footwear, safety, public transport etc. There is also an explanation of the fascinating geology which gives rise to the landscape you will see before you by Simon Conway Morris.

• The trail itself is split into 12 chapters with maps opposite the description for each route section. The distances noted at the head of each chapter should enable you to decide how far you want to travel each day. I have split the walk into 15-mile (24-km) sections which should be achievable for those who regularly walk such distances. There are few hills to climb and the going can be quite easy. If you want a more leisurely walk and intend to visit the museums and historic buildings, study the plants, animals and birds in the nature reserves and elsewhere, then covering half that distance each day will allow you to do these things. If you do, I think the experience would be much more rewarding. However, there are those who merely wish to walk the whole distance in order to keep fit, or to raise money; you may wish to cover the 15 miles (24 km) per day. Then there are runners who I understand will run twice the distance or more, enjoy the experience and cover the whole path in a much shorter time.

• The last part includes useful information, such as local transport, tourist information centres, accommodation and further reading.

The maps used in this guide are the 1:25 000 Ordnance Survey® Explorer™ or Outdoor Leisure™ series with the path shown highlighted in yellow. The status of each section of the trail, footpath bridleway or joint cycleway is shown in green underneath.

Any parts of the path that might be difficult to follow on the ground are clearly highlighted in the route description and important points to watch out for are marked with letters in each chapter, both in the text and on the maps.

Should there be any need to divert the path from the route shown in this guide, to allow for maintenance work or because the path is changed, you are advised to follow waymarks along the path.

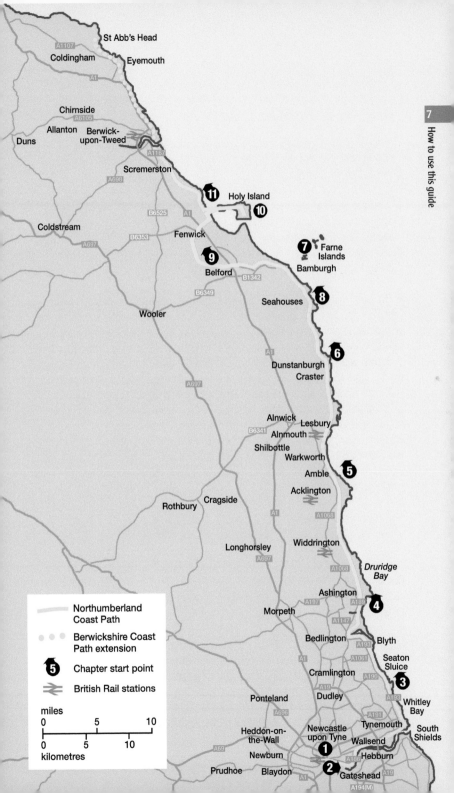

St Abb's Head

A1107 Coldingham

Eyemouth

Chirnside

A6105 Allanton

Berwick-upon-Tweed

Duns

A1167 Scremerston

A698

Coldstream

A1

B6525

A697 Fenwick

11

Holy Island

10

B6353

7 Farne Islands

Bamburgh

9

Belford B1342

B6349

Wooler

Seahouses

A1

6

Dunstanburgh Craster

A697

Alnwick Lesbury

B6341 Alnmouth

Shilbottle

Warkworth

Amble

5

Acklington

Rothbury Cragside

A1 A1068

Longhorsley

Widdrington

A697

A1068 Druridge Bay

Ashington

A197 A189

4

Morpeth A1147

Bedlington Blyth

A193

A1 A1061 Seaton Sluice

Cramlington A190

3

A19

Ponteland Dudley Whitley Bay

A696 A191 Tynemouth

Heddon-on-the-Wall

Newcastle upon Tyne Wallsend South Shields

Newburn 1

Hebburn

Prudhoe Blaydon 2 Gateshead

A194(M)

Legend:

— Northumberland Coast Path

··· Berwickshire Coast Path extension

5 Chapter start point

⇌ British Rail stations

miles
0   5   10

0   5   10
kilometres

Lindisfarne Priory.

Distance checklist

This list will assist you in calculating the distances between your proposed
overnight accommodation and in checking your progress along the walk.

Location	Approximate distance from previous location	
	miles	*km*
Newcastle and Gateshead round walk	3.5	5.6
Newcastle – Tynemouth	9.5	15
North Shields – St Mary's Lighthouse	5.7	9.4
St Mary's Lighthouse – Newbiggin-by-the-Sea	16.3	26.3
Newbiggin-by-the-Sea – Warkworth	16	26
Warkworth – Craster	13	21
Craster – Seahouses	10	16
The Farne Islands	2	3
Seahouses – Belford	11.7	18.6
Belford – Lindisfarne	9.5	15.4
Holy Island	4.2	6.8
Lindisfarne – Berwick-upon-Tweed	13.8	22
Berwick-upon-Tweed – St Abbs	14.7	23.1
St Abb's Head round walk	3.6	5.9
Approximate total	135	220

The Royal Border Bridge spans the River Tweed. This is the 7 a.m. East Coast train from London King's Cross at 11.37 a.m. on an August morning in 2012, 162 years after it was opened by Queen Victoria and Prince Albert.

PART ONE

Introduction

Coast, castles and coal mines!

Why should you walk the Northumberland Coast Path? First of all you will get to view superb scenery, some of England's most imposing castles, nearly 60 miles (97 km) of empty sandy beaches, extraordinary wild flowers and examples of the most dramatic rock formations in Europe.

This path description covers the majority of the tidal area bordering the ancient county of Northumbria. It starts from the Quayside in lively Newcastle and takes you along the River Tyne on old railway lines now bordered by incredible floral displays in spring and summer. It continues through classic seaside resorts and on to industrial areas, which are still managing to exist in an ever more competitive world.

The (Norman) New Castle at Newcastle – worth a visit.

The castles

Starting with the New Castle at Newcastle the scenery is dotted with these historic buildings all along this route. As you reach the mouth of the Tyne, the dramatic Tynemouth Castle and Priory situated on top of the red cliffs are the first major mediaeval buildings you will see on the side of the River Tyne after leaving Newcastle. The next grand building is Warkworth Castle by the River Aln, in which the castle reflects if you care to take an evening walk beside the river. At the end of the next day's walking you will start to see dramatic ruins of Dunstanburgh Castle sitting on one of the Whinstone (dolerite) outcrops. Next you will see Bamburgh Castle, the most imperial of them all, on this coast. As you come round the corner at Bamburgh you get dramatic views of the castle at Lindisfarne, and within a day's walk of Lindisfarne you will see the remnants of a once great castle at Berwick-upon-Tweed and some of the most impressive town ramparts of any in Europe.

The birds

Again starting at Newcastle you will see cormorants swimming in the River Tyne and the largest inland colony of kittiwakes in England on and around the Tyne Bridge. They go down to the North Sea in the late evening and at dawn, when sand eels come near to the surface, and breed in the city centre. In winter a few linger and give any herring gulls a rough time. The rest are probably out at sea. You will see

Kittiwakes nest on the Tyne Bridge and the coastal cliffs.

more kittiwakes on the way along the River Tyne down to the sea. Take care as you go under the Tyne Bridge in spring and summer!

Along the seafronts of Tynemouth and Whitley Bay there are thankfully rather fewer herring gulls to steal your fish and chips than at many resorts. As you encounter the rocky bays beyond St Mary's Lighthouse you will start to see the first eider ducks.

After Blyth you have to cross several river estuaries where wading birds, ring plovers and oyster catchers can be seen all year round, with an influx of wintering birds from Scandinavia if you are walking this way between October and March. When you arrive at Druridge Bay, lakes created by open-cast coal mining provide homes for egrets, herons and a host of wetland waterfowl, which you can view from

hides at the Low Hauxley nature reserve of the Northumberland Wildlife Trust. The Farne Islands are stunning between the months of May and July when large numbers of auks, that is puffins, razorbills and guillemots, come to nest on the islands, which are managed by the National Trust. You must spend at least a day and take a boat trip out to these islands for a walk. If you are visiting the area as a pilgrim, then Inner Farne as well as Lindisfarne will be of particular interest. Further north you will see more waders in the bay at Lindisfarne and can catch glimpses of the gannets on their fishing trips from Bass Rock in the Firth of Forth. This isolated volcanic plug, now swathed in white, will come into sight of at the end of the walk.

The flowers

The dramatic display starts you off on the railway line just downstream from

Newcastle Quayside if you follow the main cycleway just after setting out. I'm told that the reason why flowers grow here in such profusion is that the soil is too poor to support grass. They were apparently planted here as seeds soon after the establishment of the walkway/cycleway and are now flourishing. The next big displays of wild flowers are in Northumberland's coastal dunes, which start at Whitley Bay. There are around 100 miles (160 km) of dunes along the coast of Northumberland. All of them have some rare flowers and butterflies in them. The greatest profusions occur in the managed nature reserves, which I shall mention as you continue the walk.

The views

The views which you'll see walking along this coast are outstanding. Because the ground is relatively flat you should have beautiful skies. In addition,

if the weather does hold, you will see for long distances and become familiar with the principle landmarks. When you look back and see one of these markers, and see how far away it is, you'll be proud of yourself for having walked so far in such a short time.

The industrial archaeology

The Northumberland coast is a great place for industrial archaeology. The coal on which much of it sits is the foundation for the wealth of the area. From the 13th to the 20th century this area was supplying coal to most of Britain. There are records of Newcastle coal being supplied to Corfe Castle in Dorset in the 13th century. As the coal became harder to extract, ingenuity was required to mine it. The miners progressed into engineers and began to develop ways for getting around such problems. First of all they started excavating deeper. They then had to transport the coal

further to the coast in order to ship it to the rest of the country. This led to the Northumbrian trackways and eventually to the foundation of the railways. The world's first functional and commercial passenger transporting railway systems were developed by Robert Stephenson in Newcastle. His father, George Stephenson, began building locomotives near the colliery where he started his career as a brakesman before going on to become an engineer looking after the static steam engines. Amongst many other projects, the Stephenson firm went on to build the Alexandria–Cairo Railway and the Liverpool and Manchester Railway, including the construction of the bridges which took their railway over the River Tyne at Newcastle and the River Tweed at Berwick.

Other notable creators from the area include Joseph Swan, who invented the first electric lamp in Newcastle, and Mosley Street was the first in the

Newcastle Quayside.

Introduction

world to be lit by electric lamps. Then came William Armstrong who perfected the hydraulic system which is still used throughout the world. His most famous project is the Swing Bridge in Newcastle, built to allow a factory to be established upstream of the 18th-century Stone Bridge. Without this new bridge the export of products – from entire ships to new gun systems – to the farthest parts of the world would have been hindered. Armstrong was also responsible for designing and constructing the hydraulic mechanism

Dunstanburgh Castle, near Craster, built by a rebelling noble to annoy the king of England, with later additions by John of Gaunt.

The North Sea Trail logo, a white wave.

which opens London's Tower Bridge. The Woodhorn and Discovery museums cover all this admirably, and should be included in your visit.

The achievement

If you walk the whole distance you will be immensely proud of the achievement. You will also have a thorough knowledge of this part of the north-east of England. If you are sponsored you will have the achievement of raising funds for your favourite organisation. If you are raising funds for the RNLI you may get a good welcome as you pass their offices along the coast.

The knowledge you will gain if you walk this path slowly and inspect the many sites along its route, find out how they came to be there and how they have survived in this region, will stay with you for years to come. You will really get to know the wonderful north-east of England.

What's this path like?

The first 30 miles (48 km) of this route, which might take two or three days, almost exclusively follows the two routes of the National Cycle Network, Hadrian's (route 72), and Coast and Castles (route 1). Much of this route is paved like a small country lane with a line down the middle (which everybody seems to ignore) to divide pedestrians and cyclists. This is not a problem. Much of it is quiet and cyclists are frequent enough that pedestrians are aware they need to take some care. The walking and cycling fraternity can enjoy each other's company and stay in the same sort of accommodation, where special facilities are often available – such as drying rooms – for the followers of both sports.

Through the seaside resorts cyclists and pedestrians quite often share the seafront, also not a problem. Faster cyclists take to the road at these points, whilst families and slower cyclists can enjoy the traffic-free seafront. On many sections golfers will be around to greet you. There are some old and excellent golf courses all the way along. Their clubhouses sometimes welcome walkers, and can be a good place to have a snack, park the car, or have a drink. Just ask.

Detailed information is given in the guide section of this book to enable you to follow roads which have pavements alongside where the cycleway is on the road. In a couple of places the cycleway is next to a busy road but entirely separate from it. This means that they are quite safe, although they can be a bit noisy at times. Those who wish to have the satisfaction of walking the whole of this coast must be prepared to follow these sections that cross the rivers and main roads, but are easily traversed on foot.

After Lynemouth, pedestrians have to take to the pavements for a few miles via Ellington and reach Cresswell. From Cresswell to St Abbs there are rights of way that are linked together to form the Northumberland Coast Path and the Berwickshire Coast Path. A few of these rights of way can be muddy, flooded, overgrown, unmarked and almost impassable. Most, especially the main parts, which are right on the coast, make pleasant walking. Some sections, particularly those looked after by the National Trust, Natural England, the Howick Estate and some of the golf clubs (in particular the Royal Bamburgh) are beautifully maintained. I shall comment on this in the text so that you can decide whether you still want to face the challenge of walking the whole route. If not, you may choose to skip the poorly maintained parts and enjoy the best by taking the bus now and again.

In Scotland the path is all well waymarked, in some parts skillfully engineered, and the only problem I encountered was just north of Burnmouth where the path was rather overgrown. The path up to that point had, however, been cleared and I think I had just beaten the clearance team to the last section that day. The cliffs are larger there, but you stay on the top much of the time, so climbing and descending is minimal. You will still need good boots for this section.

Please note that, excluding Chapter 1, ascents and descents for each chapter have been omitted due to the variations: depending on which sand dune you decide to go round or over, or whether you decide to take to the beach!

What else will you see?

You will see the end of Hadrian's Wall in the town that is appropriately called Wallsend. You can walk or cycle along the seafront for some nine or so miles (15 km) to the small island of St Mary's with its imposing lighthouse you can walk to at low tide. The proud towns of Newcastle, and the more recently created North Tyneside district, provide you with lots of wayside information as you go along. The whole of this section is really well signed. The engineering standards are faultless, and footwear can be anything you find comfortable for all-day walking. Once north of St Mary's a well-marked and surfaced path takes you along the cliffs to Seaton Sluice, which now comes under the jurisdiction of the unitary Northumberland County Council. It all becomes more rural, but still has history and beautiful sights to remember.

Puffin with sand eels on Staple Island.

Safety

Footwear

From Newcastle to St Mary's Lighthouse you can wear anything that is comfortable; sandals, light shoes, walking boots, anything goes. After that there are sections through fields and muddy tracks, so good waterproof walking boots are recommended. On the official inland route between Seahouses and Belford there is often very deep mud, after rain the paths flood, and either wellies or combat boots from an army surplus store, plus waterproof socks, would be essential unless there been has been a drought. If you don't like the sound of that walk from Seahouses to Bamburgh along the beach at low tide, walk onto Beadnell Bay across the Bamburgh Castle Golf Club, and take the bus to Fenwick Granary where there is a bus stop at the end of the lane.

Then you can walk down to the coast and, at low tide (plan carefully), cross the Lindisfarne Causeway. You must first have studied the tide tables available online, onsite and in all the tourist information centres.

Tides

The tides run extremely fast up and down this coast. All warning signs should be heeded. In the unlikely event that you will be bathing in the North Sea, check the tides and all safety warnings first. It would be sensible to look at the tide tables, which can now be obtained online, before walking along the beach in long stretches. This is unlikely to be dangerous around the sand dunes since retreat should be easy, but not ideal. River crossings are not advised.

Take no risks on the Lindisfarne Causeway. There are sections just south

Converted fishing boats waiting to take passengers out to the Farne Islands at Seahouses.

of the causeway, where the mud makes the beach more or less inaccessible, that certainly as far as Bamburgh you should have no serious problems. I would only advise walking the sandy beaches. The rocky ones can be interesting for their geology and their rock pools but walking any distance could be painful. On beaches where they are divided by cliffs it is advised not to try to walk between each beach at any time. These are the main places where the emergency services have to be called in to rescue people trapped by the tides.

Mobile communications

It is advisable to remember that mobile phones do not work on considerable stretches of this coast. Hence the advice is to take some form of an audible warning, such as a whistle. If you are walking alone it is advisable to tell someone where you expect to be at the end of each walk so they can raise the alarm should you not appear.

Personal safety

Crime rates have been falling rapidly in recent years. Northumbria Police force carries out patrols on the path along the River Tyne and they keep a watchful eye on what is going on along the rest of the coast. In Newcastle and Gateshead there is an effective police presence. Northumbria police have a 101 number, which you can ring to report any incident which you feel they should know about. All the police I came across on the route were helpful and asked if everything was all right. Obviously you have to take care of your personal possessions as you would anywhere. When riots were

The Newcastle Quayside Sunday market.

gripping other English cities south of this conurbation in 2011, reports in the local papers record that the Geordies were watching films in the pedestrian squares and generally having a good night out.

Finding your way

You will have to refer to this guide to follow this path. Most smartphones now have GPS and this can be useful in locating where you are if you think you have gone off the route. There are some apps which are recommended in the Useful Information section at the back of this book, which furnish you with a map; once installed, this means you do not have to rely on any mobile indications whilst you're following the path. (There are also apps listed for tide times and one which shows all cycle routes in Great Britain.)

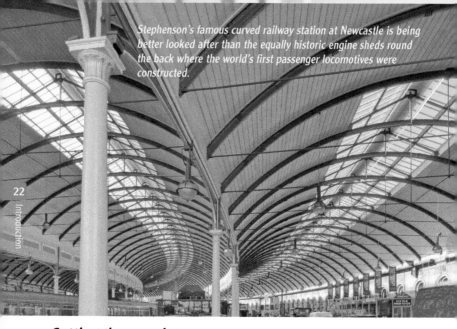

Stephenson's famous curved railway station at Newcastle is being better looked after than the equally historic engine sheds round the back where the world's first passenger locomotives were constructed.

Getting there and getting around

Newcastle Gateshead has excellent communications. The airport has national and international services. The railway services to Newcastle, Berwick-upon-Tweed and Alnmouth stations are fast and frequent from all parts of mainland UK. There is a ferry service, daily in each direction, from Holland.

The cheapest way to get there is to buy up to 90 days in advance online. There are direct services from London, all of which call at Newcastle and many of which stop in Berwick.

The 'Coaster' bus service covers the area from Gateshead by Newcastle to Whitley Bay. This enables you to be based anywhere in that area and cover sections of the path each day at your leisure. There is also a frequent bus service from Newcastle to Blyth.

Newbiggin is served by express services from Newcastle via Ashington, although that's not much use reaching other parts of the path. Go online after looking at the bus info in Useful Information to check the latest position on buses.

For the section of the path between Berwick and Amble there is a bus service that calls at all the main points mentioned in this book, which could enable you to base yourself at Berwick or some other settlement along the route, doing a part of the walk each day in that area.

There is also a service from Berwick to Lindisfarne which links at Beal with the Coast and Castles buses between Newcastle and Berwick. North of Berwick there is a reliable bus service between Berwick, Coldingham and St Abbs.

That covers the whole of the route. Details of all these bus services as they stand at the time of writing are in the Useful Information section at the back.

The geology of the Northumbrian coast

Simon Conway Morris

To the untrained eye the Coast Path winds its way between the sometimes tempestuous North Sea and an open landscape that abuts the sea as dune-flanked beaches, open estuaries or rugged cliffs. The geologist sees a different dimension. Over the relatively short distance of 108 miles (174 km) there is evidence for the closure of an ocean, the accumulation of enough coal to power industry and warm homes for centuries, an episode of massive igneous activity and an ice age. These various events span an interval of some 430 million years (Ma) and the migration by continental drift of this part of the world from a position well south of the equator to its present location at about 55°N.

For nearly its entire length the Coast Path traverses rocks deposited during the Carboniferous Period (c. 300-340 Ma). The geological story, however, extends back another 100 Ma because adjacent to St Abb's Head there are Silurian (Llandovery) sediments. These were deposited on the margin of a long-vanished ocean (known as Iapetus) and as the tectonic plate descended beneath the ancient continent of Laurentia these sediments were effectively plastered against the continental margin. The actual line of closure of the Iapetus Ocean is now deeply concealed beneath younger rocks, but lies a little to the south of the Farne Islands.

Thereafter England and Scotland were never to be sundered, at least geologically. Our story resumes with evidence from the Devonian (c. 410 Ma), where St Abb's Head itself is composed of volcanic rocks, with some similar examples outcropping towards Eyemouth. A little south of this town we enter (or leave) Carboniferous territory that then extends almost without interruption to Newcastle. Very broadly the Carboniferous is divided into a lower unit, succeeded by the Millstone Grit and ultimately the Coal Measures. So walking south one moves successively upwards in geological time. The earlier sequences are mostly marine (as is evident from fossils like corals and brachiopods). Land, however, is not far away and periodic emergence is marked by coal seams. One or two were economically viable but their importance was dwarfed by the Coal Measures that extend south from Alnmouth. Pits were not only scattered across the country but in places workings extended far beyond the shore. The productive seams, which were up to

The whole of this coast consists of long sandy beaches, massive dunes and weird and wonderful rock formations.

St Abbs harbour seen from St Abb's Head, with Eyemouth beyond the far side of the bay; one of the richest marine wildlife reserves in Britain.

8 feet thick, comprise only a small fraction of the sedimentary sequence. Typically this shows a cyclical pattern and crustal movements combined with the shifting river channels of immense deltaic systems led to recurrent accumulation of sands, muds and peat mires. Situated on the equator this was a lush and thickly vegetated world, although on occasion the sea invaded and left a calling card in the form of so-called marine bands.

Towards the end of the Carboniferous (c. 300 Ma) a massive intrusion of igneous rock in the form of quartz-dolerite produced both the celebrated Whin Sill and a set of associated dyke swarms that cut across the Carboniferous rocks. Once completely buried, uplift and erosion now reveal exposures across northern England, allowing some estimate of the vast volume of once molten rock, perhaps exceeding 50 cubic miles. Its resistance shows, forming as it does the Farne Islands and the foundations of Bamburgh Castle. A major off-shoot traverses Holy Island and it is no accident that both the monastery and castle benefit from the related topography.

Hundreds of millions of years were to elapse before we can pick up the threads of the Coast Path geology. This is because much of the area is mantled by boulder clay, deposited beneath the ice sheets that covered northern Britain until about 20,000 years ago. As the glaciers retreated so vast quantities of meltwater sands and gravels accumulated, especially along the river valleys. For the walker this glacial landscape may pass almost unnoticed, but no visitor can fail to be struck by the dunes that stretch along many parts of the coast. They began to form about 6,000 years ago, with sand derived from off-shore and still maintained by the persistent on-shore winds. Some of these dunes can be found on Holy Island, but here even more striking is the superb sweep of the sands and the almost magical quality of this remote place.

The North Sea Trail is partly funded by the European Union under the Interreg IIIB North Sea Programme.

The aim is to create a series of footpaths around the North Sea coast to enable people to enjoy walking in these coastal landscapes and, at the same time, to discover the special aspects of these places - what makes them different and what gives them a common North Sea culture.

As well as creating and regenerating footpaths, the Programme is working to improve access to many heritage features. It is also working with the business community to ensure that the economies of these areas will benefit from the North Sea Trail and that the tourist industry will provide added value to the North Sea Trail experience.

In some areas, the footpaths are well developed, in others they are still being created.

Twenty-six regions in Norway, Sweden, Denmark, Germany, the Netherlands and the United Kingdom are involved in creating this path.

In conjunction with the North Sea Cycle Trail, the major part of the tidal coast of old Northumberland is now accessible to pedestrians. Lively riverside scenes, sedate Victorian seaside resorts, miles of beautiful flower-covered dunes, sandy beaches, dramatic cliffs and castles all await you. The existence of this through-route is a closely guarded secret but this book gives you the information needed to identify where the path is and how it can be found from Newcastle Quayside to St Abbs, just over the Scottish border. Other guides will be needed if you want to continue to Edinburgh and beyond.

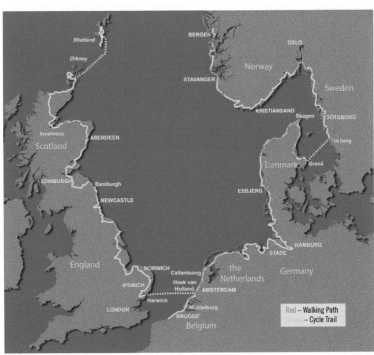

Berwick Bridge was opened a few years after King James VI of Scotland, newly James I of England (he of the Bible), expressed his displeasure at having to cross a wooden bridge between his two kingdoms in 1603.

PART TWO

Northumberland
Coast Path

Newcastle and Gateshead round walk

A round tour of Newcastle and Gateshead riverside

3.5 miles (5.6 km)

Ascents n/a
Descents 350 feet (100 metres)
Highest point The railway: 120 feet (37 metres) above high water on the river
Lowest point 17 feet (5 metres)

A gentle introduction to the area, on pages 36 – 40 the Route Description suggests a short circuit around Newcastle to get your bearings and to see the location of the main sites in a brisk one-hour walk. During this you will come across some of the major landmarks so that you can orientate yourself for the rest of your visit. These are lettered A – Z and AA – AC on the map opposite and the maps accompanying pages, 36 – 40. The same system is used throughout the book. Before you begin your journey, there is also a brief history of the main characters and buildings that are most relevant to your future walk on the North Sea Trail to and along the north-eastern coast of England. The tour starts (and finishes) the walk at the Newcastle Railway Station but you can obviously start at any point around the circuit.

Things to look out for

The Discovery Museum **W** has first-class exhibitions, which you should most definitely not miss. To reach it walk west from the station. Turn left coming out of the station and cross the road at some point. Continue west along this road (Westmorland Road) until you see a very large red brick building with copper domes or cupolas on each corner. This was the Co-operative distribution centre. Horses and carts used to go right in, stock up on the loading platforms, which you will walk along to see the exhibitions, and set off to their shops in the area.

Now it's the Discovery Museum. I recommend a visit to prepare for walking the North Sea Trail/ Northumberland Coast Path because everything you see along the way will make much more sense as part of the history of the area. When you see a derelict shipyard or factory by the Tyne or a closed railway or coal mine site in one of the coastal small towns and villages, you will understand its importance in the historical order of things, instead of just seeing dead unused structures. You will also be able to picture it as it was in the past.

The entrance to the museum is on the far, right-hand side. Entrance is free. Say 'hullo' nicely to the staff inside and make for the far end, past *Turbinia*, once the world's fastest ship.

Go to floor one and look right for the 'Story of the Tyne' exhibition. Turn left inside the room and look at the model,

Map letters refer
mainly to the Route
Description of a walk
around Newcastle on
pages 36 – 40.

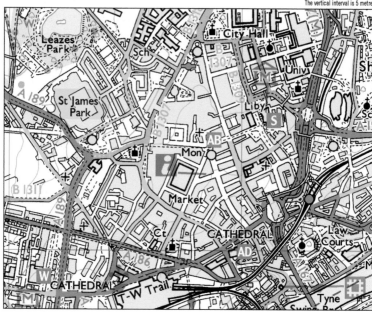

which graphically shows the first stage of your walk along the River Tyne. This model shows the river and its environs between here and Tynemouth.

If you make a study of this model, or even take a 1904 Ordnance Survey map with you on the walk, the whole area could come to life in your mind. A busy river, as busy as the road you will come alongside on day one is now. Imagine thousands of workers going to work by train every morning, the smoke, the noise, the terraced houses – many of which survive – occupied by those ship workers and the slightly bigger, semi or fully detached houses, which the managers and engineers would have rented. The competition between British shipyards to get the contracts, produce the goods on time, and produce the biggest and the best was enormous.

On the model, look at all the hundreds of wagonways which brought coal direct from the mines to the staithes, where it was tipped onto the ships and sent all over Britain. From this coal came the wealth, which paid for the massive engineering projects and for the new universities. It also paid for the Literary and Philosophical Institute you saw on your quick tour, where young men studied and others heard the lectures from the thinkers and engineers who invented the steam railway locomotive, a safe miners' lamp (the Geordie) and the world's first electric lamps. They then went on to develop technology for the car, the lorry and the planes, all of which Britain still produces. Later on the walk I shall recommend a visit to the Woodhorn Museum, a twenty-minute walk inland from the Coast Path just south of Newbiggin, where the coal mines will be brought to life for you.

The second display at the Discovery Museum is an interesting analysis of the problems that engineers and thinkers in this area had to resolve, and the solutions they came up with. It's called 'Tyneside Challenge' and is at the entrance to the hall, on level one. So come out of the 'Story of the Tyne' exhibition and walk to the other end of the northern gallery.

The Laing Art Gallery S will also give you a taste of what you will see both in the city of Newcastle and at many places along the coast to the north. There are beautiful historic paintings showing the city through the ages, the coastal scenery and people enjoying themselves in the seaside towns you will walk through. To get there from the station go up Grainger Street to the Monument AB, and bear right down New Bridge Street, towards and across John Dobson Street, making for the domed building which is the Laing Art Gallery. On the outside west wall is a mural depicting one of the Cullercoats seaside views.

Make for the 'Northern Spirit' exhibition. The first display that will catch your eye might be Bewick's wood engravings along with his wood blocks. There are also many local skillfully crafted works on display in a wide range of materials. The main reason for suggesting that the interested walker should look at this gallery is the variety of paintings which show the city, and the Northumbrian coast, through the ages. The works of the famous Cullercoats artists, which are on display in this gallery, are a must-see if you are walking this coast.

For centuries everything in Newcastle and Gateshead happened on the riverside. Traders brought goods from other countries, coal went out on the coal boats and ballast was unloaded on the 'Ballast Hills' just downstream. (Many of the boats came empty, so had

Pictures and objects that will really add to your experience as you walk through Newcastle as well as along the Coast Path.

LAING ART GALLERY

to carry quantities of ballast, which was dumped here, before returning to sea with the coal.) During the unsettled times before the union with Scotland, a town wall was assiduously maintained to protect the inhabitants and their wealth. The wall ran right round the town with the harbour just outside it, as it still is in Berwick.

The riverside 'chares', or alleyways, are thought to have been piers with boats alongside them. This changed when a harbour wall was built in a long straight line beside the river, as it still is here. At first the merchants lived in the grand houses near the Newcastle Quayside. The Surtees' house Z, which you saw on the quick tour, would have been one such house, and remains as a well preserved example. Eventually this area became too smelly and smoky to be pleasant to live in and the merchants moved out of town. When the High Level Bridge was completed with easy road and rail access to the top of the hill the riverside lost out on both sides of the river as the place to be. In Victorian times the emphasis was on the area now occupied by Grainger Town. Grand houses, grand shops and grand offices all designed in the 19th century. The great fire of Newcastle and Gateshead, started by a warehouse fire on 6 October 1854, blasted and burned the slums that occupied the riverside out of existence and the stone façades of the shipping companies' offices replaced the old half-timbered façades. The exhibition 'Northern Spirit' gives a fascinating and often beautiful idea of this whole progression of the city. Don't miss it.

The Robert Stephenson and Company Works AC is, at the time of writing, still standing with its blue plaque behind Newcastle Railway Station in New Street, off Forth Street, behind the postal sorting office. This is the birthplace of the British Industrial Revolution. In this building, where the founding fathers created the means by which Britain, for better or for worse, managed to move its troops, imperial staff, food and equipment on every continent in the world. It may at the moment still be viewed from without, but looks very vulnerable between the anonymous blocks that surround it.

The Stephensons

George Stephenson was the son of a pumping engine fireman at a Northumberland colliery 10 miles (16 km) west of Newcastle, born in 1781. Education was out of reach in youth but at 17 he began a job as an engineman and at 20 became a brakesman – the person who controls the winding gear at the pithead. He had realised that education would enable him to get on. He made shoes and mended clocks to earn extra money. George and his wife Fanny moved to Willington Quay where they lived in one room and Robert was born in 1803. They moved to Killingworth, about 5 miles north of Byker. After a brief spell working over the Scottish border he returned to work in Killingworth. When one of the engines failed he was called in to fix it. He succeeded in this to such an extent that he was promoted to enginewright and became the local expert on steam-powered equipment. He went on to develop a miners' safety lamp, which became known as a 'Geordie', said by some to be the reason why the residents of this area are proud to be Geordies to this day.

Steam locomotives were being used in Northumbrian collieries after their inventor Richard Trevithick made one for a local mine owner. George Stephenson was one of a number of local men who started to work on their own designs and began producing engines in a workshop near his home, Dial House, named for the dial on the front following from his interest in clocks. He went on to build the famous 'Locomotion' for the Stockton and Darlington Railway. The company director was considering powering the new line with horses. Stephenson persuaded him to try steam, and the two men subsequently set up the firm Robert Stephenson and Company, with George's son Robert as company director and Michael Longridge of the Bedlington Ironworks, where the wrought iron rails were to be made, as the fourth partner.

It was George Stephenson who saw that a standard gauge would be needed if all these lines were eventually to link and form a system. He decided on 4 feet 8.5 inches (1.435 metres), which has since become the standard gauge for western Europe, America, China and quite a few more countries around the world. It was George Stephenson who went on to be the key member of the team who constructed and successfully opened the world's first passenger railway, the Liverpool and Manchester Railway. The opening ceremony was attended by the Prime Minister and the Duke of Wellington, with eight trains made in the Newcastle works leading on the opening day.

The Armstrongs

The engineer William George Armstrong had established the Elswick works at Newcastle just upstream of the bridges in 1847. He is most famous for the invention of the breech loading gun but companies with the Armstrong name went on to make motorcars (Armstrong Siddeley cars were still around well into the 1960s) and in 1913 an aerial department started building planes. In addition to the boats built for the Russian Trans-Siberian Railway, boats were built for the Japanese, Russian and American navies. The company also built the world's first polar icebreaker. In 1912, when Armstrong started making ships that were too big to go through the swing bridge, ship building was moved to Walker and the imperial navies of Japan and Russia were amongst the customers.

One of the most intriguing projects was to build two boats intended to transport people across Lake Baikal before the total completion of the Trans-Siberian Railway. Lake Baikal is the deepest freshwater lake in the world at nearly one mile deep and contains the largest body of fresh water in the world, approximately one fifth of the world's total fresh water.

The Russians were aiming to link the Siberian Empire with Moscow and needed a supply route that could reduce the dependency of their population on imports from China and the Far East. In addition, the Japanese were threatening the Empire's eastern frontiers, and the Russians needed to get troops and supplies through as quickly as possible. The Trans-Siberian Railway was successfully completed towards the end of the 19th century but Lake Baikal still had to be crossed. Initially they laid railway tracks across the lake on the solid ice. Unfortunately there were undiscovered hot springs underneath part of the route and one of the first trains disappeared beneath the ice. General Makarov of the Imperial Army designed two ice-breaking steamships, which would connect the Trans-Siberian Railway across Lake Baikal.

The train ferry SS *Baikal* was built in Elswick in 1897 and the passenger and package freight steamer SS *Angara* was built in 1900 based upon the general study of similar ice-breaking vessels on the American Great Lakes. He chose Armstrong Whitworth in Newcastle upon Tyne to build ships. They were built in kit form and sent to Lake Baikal for reassembly. The *Baikal* had 15 boilers, four funnels, could carry 24 railway coaches and a locomotive and was 210 feet (64 metres) long. The *Angara* was smaller with two funnels. The *Baikal* did not survive the revolution, but the *Angara* is still around and is currently moored in Irkutsk on Lake Baikal, open to the public as a museum. It may now be the oldest steam icebreaker in the world.

The ice-breaking ship Baikal, *built in kit form in Scotswood, Newcastle, and taken to Lake Baikal in Siberia for assembly.*

John Scott, 1st Earl of Eldon KC PC FRS FSA

John Scott and Betty Surtees eloped with the help of a friend who supplied the ladder, from the first floor window of the now famous house. They rode post-haste to Black Shields in Scotland. After a distinguished career in London he became the first Earl of Eldon. His country seat is at Encombe, on the South West Coast Path in Dorset. Lord Encombe was one of the subsidiary titles. Eldon was a colliery village, which the family owned in County Durham. The whole story of his and the Surtees family, gives a fascinating insight into the historical development of Newcastle's wealth, political power and development in the 18th and 19th centuries. I'm not sure what he would have thought of the Eldon shopping centre.

The Cathedrals

The Anglican Cathedral is much like a large mediaeval church in any town or village in England. It has a pleasant design with the various centuries intermingling well together, and the one remarkable feature that is unusual in England is the lantern, known as a Scottish crown. There are, however, a number of memorials to the characters who played a part in making Newcastle what it is, or played a major role in the history of England or Britain.

First inside the door is a memorial to Collingwood. Every schoolchild in this country is or was told about Nelson putting his telescope to his blind eye, his heroic death and being brought back to English shores in a barrel of brandy (not rum). Not so many of us remember that the person who took over command was Collingwood, who went on to win the battle, which was decisive in shaping the whole future of Britain in Europe. He was a local lad, and you will see his column at Tynemouth, with him looking out to sea. His life was a rather sad story of being compelled at the end of his career to stay on at work until he died in harness and at sea, but read the monument text to see that they put as positive a version as they could at the time. He is buried in Westminster Abbey alongside his friend and colleague Nelson.

During his leave from the navy he loved to go for long walks. The story goes that he always carried in his pockets a few acorns. When he reached a spot where he thought an oak would grow well he would heel an acorn into the ground, so that Britain's navy would have enough oak for its naval ships in centuries to follow. Some of these oaks may still be around. Something to look for on your long walk.

Also at the back of the Anglican Cathedral are memorials to various members of the Ridley family. Read the wording of them thoroughly and bear in mind that the reader is meant to emulate such superlative qualities. You will hear more about this distinguished family when we get near to one of their estates at Blyth in a few days' time. There is also, on the north wall, a memorial to Councillor Mosley, after whom the world's first electrically lit street is named.

One other gem which might appeal to the more curious visitor is a small piece of blackened wood hanging in a frame on the south wall, with a letter from a Dorset vicar explaining its origin and importance to a 19th century Dorset rector. The object concerns a piece of Newcastle's Roman history and the original Roman bridge over the Tyne. This is where the Swing Bridge now stands.

The Catholic Cathedral B was, like the Anglican one, originally built as a parish church. A Swiss family called Pugin had left France at the time of the revolution and settled in England. Auguste Pugin was a gifted artist and gave lessons in architectural drawing to paying pupils, which his son Augustus also attended. The father was particularly well known for his architectural drawings of famous Gothic buildings in Britain and France. Augustus, however, decided having had a successful career in design to go to sea and became a ship's captain. He was shipwrecked in 1830 off Leith, where he met the Edinburgh architect James Graham, who persuaded him to give up sailing and develop his career as an architect. He converted to Catholicism in 1834 and became the leading advocate of an ornate neo-Gothic style. He designed this church, which later became a cathedral, as well as many churches of both denominations in England, Ireland and Australia. His most famous work was the design of the interior of the new Palace of Westminster, the House of Commons, in London. Many architects were highly critical of his style at the time, but take a look, a very thorough restoration has just been completed.

The New Castle P is the fortification which gave Newcastle it's name. On the site of a Roman fortification guarding their bridgehead on the Tyne, Robert, son of William the Conqueror, built a wooden structure, which came to be called the New Castle, in 1080. The stone castle was built in the late 12th century and the Black Gate added in the 13th. A visit to the Laing Art Gallery will show how it looked over the centuries. Good views are from Bottle Bank, Gateshead, and you can catch glimpses of it from the Sage, the Gateshead Millennium Bridge and the Newcastle Railway Station.

A trip down the Tyne

If one of the larger boats is setting off for Tynemouth with a blue badge guide there is a rewarding trip to be had, lasting about three hours. You can wander around on deck and get your bearings for the beginning of the long walk. You may well see harbour seals at Tynemouth, and you will see a range of riverside activities and have them all explained to you. Do be aware that the smaller boats are encased in glass and sometimes run without an accredited guide. Opportunities for photography are limited, and the whole experience is more like a coach trip than a cruise. Details of the cruises are posted on the Quayside by the boat moorings, just downstream from the Millennium Bridge. The timetables are quite complicated, so take care to get the day and time right.

Route description

Come out of Newcastle Railway Station A and turn right after looking

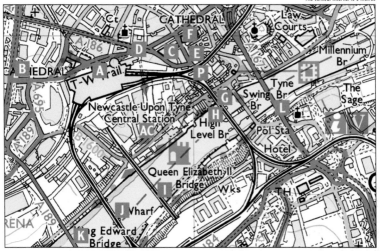

left at the tall spire of the Catholic Cathedral B across the road. The main building (not the spire) was designed by the architect responsible for the interior of the House of Commons, Augustus Welby Northmore Pugin. Go past the Literary and Philosophical Institute C where the site of the route of Emperor Hadrian's Roman Wall is marked in red on the pavement in front behind the railings. Very briefly look across the street to the north and note the statue of George Stephenson D. Fork right down Westgate Street parallel with the railway and until you see ahead of you the mediaeval main gate to the Castle, the Black Gate E, and the unusual 15th-century lantern tower of the Newcastle Anglican Cathedral F on your left. Go through the railway arch on your right (note the many iron rivets that hold this structure together) and to the right of the Bridge Hotel G. There you will see the road entrance to Robert Stephenson's recently restored cast iron High Level Bridge H. No rivets here, but solid iron sections cast in a

foundry and bolted together, a world first in bridge design on this scale. Note that the railway from London is above the road. This was the world's first combined road and rail bridge and was opened by Queen Victoria in 1849.

Weather permitting you will get superb views from this bridge of the River Tyne and the six other bridges which cross it at this point. Use the left-hand, eastern pavement of the bridge. You are 100 feet (30 metres) above the River Tyne, a good viewpoint. Look upstream to see the nearest, blue railway bridge, the Queen Elizabeth II Bridge I, part of the Metro transport system. Beyond that the King Edward Bridge J, built when the High Level Bridge reached rail capacity during the early 20th-century. Upstream of that is the Redheugh (road) Bridge K, built to reduce congestion on the famous London to Edinburgh Great North Road Tyne Bridge L that had become overloaded, as the public took to their cars later in the 20th-century.

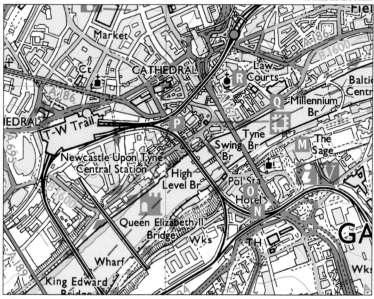

Looking downstream and east towards the North Sea is, immediately below you, the 19th-century red and white Swing Bridge, beyond that the dramatic curves of the 20th-century Foster and Partners-designed glass structure called the Sage M, which you will be visiting in a few minutes. Continue across the High Level Bridge and along Wellington Street. The shops and cafés on your left were originally underneath Gateshead Railway

Dawn view of Gateshead from Newcastle:
The Sage on the left and Gateshead's central
re-development on the right.

Front to rear: the Swing Bridge, Tyne Bridge and Gateshead Millenium Bridge.

Station. At the end of Wellington Street go left under the railway bridge and down Halfmoon Lane. Keep the yellow sandstone Central Inn N on your right. Then turn left again and down the hill past Curzon Place and down Bottle Bank past the 'Welcome to Gateshead Quays' sign. You are making for the church tower and the glass-clad Sage building on the far side of the Tyne Bridge, which you will go underneath.

Now cross Bottle Bank by the central reservation and past James Hill's fiddle O. James Hill was a popular fiddler on the streets and in the pubs in this area from 1845 to 1852.

Look ahead and across the River Tyne for good views of the bridges, the New Castle P (which you must visit later), both cathedrals, the fish market on the quay between the Swing Bridge and the High Level Bridge and, on the skyline, St James's Park, Newcastle United's stadium. Keep on towards the river to the first road crossing. Then either take the steps that lead up to the left of the church or take the street to the right of the church until you come to the Sage. The entrance to the church is nearest the riverside. On the north

wall of the church graveyard is a record of the 1854 fire and explosion and a pile of stones, which landed on the roof during the disaster.

Just before going through the Sage look across to the Newcastle Quayside Q and assess the buildings on the far side.

The tall building with the Dutch gables has a notice telling you that all the ports were dealt with by that shipping office. Remember to have a look when you are over there. Behind the eccentric domed building at the right (eastern) end of the 19th-century façades is the old Trinity House. The long building where the theatre, pubs and offices are now situated was its rigging loft. Unfortunately the beautiful ancient chapel within is only open on special heritage days a few times a year. The stone-steepled church is All Saints R and was built in the 19th century after the collapse of the mediaeval structure. When you cross the river you can read the blue plaques. If you visit the Laing Art Gallery S you will see how it all looked in the past.

The Sage is open at all reasonable hours and has eating and toilet

The Joseph Rank flour mill built in 1950 to replace capacity lost during WWII, now a comtemporary art exhibition space.

facilities. It is named after the software company that has been a major success for Gateshead's post-industrial development, and it is all about music.

You'll see that there is an enormous range of activities for people of all ages who wish to play music themselves, learn to sing or play a musical instrument, or come to hear others making music. The activities not only take place within the building but are also led by the organisation through its arts reach activities. Northern Sinfonia, one of Britain's world-class classical orchestras, hold regular concerts here. The Sage has superb acoustics and you can usually buy concert tickets at quite short notice if the programme appeals to you.

Take time to look at the Newcastle Quayside from here.

You may want to take a rest or just enjoy the view from the terrace before exiting at the other end of the building towards the Gateshead Millennium Bridge T.

As you leave the Sage note the large building on your right, which was a flourmill built in 1950. Now it hosts a range of contemporary arts activities and houses a collection of modern art installations, and is known as the Baltic Centre U. As you cross the Gateshead Millennium Bridge notice the building straight ahead, this was originally a quayside warehouse for the Co-operative Society. This was the first reinforced concrete building built in Britain and was constructed by the French company Mouchel. It is now the Malmaison Hotel V. It is nothing like as elaborate as the red brick and copper-domed building they used as their distribution centre just west of the station. This now houses the Discovery Museum W, which is a must.

After coming off the Gateshead Millennium Bridge turn left along the Quayside. Keep going until you have passed under the Tyne Bridge and admired the carving of Neptune reclining, attended by fishwives and the iron seahorses which embellish the Old Fish Market X. When you get to the still-active fish market at North Shields,

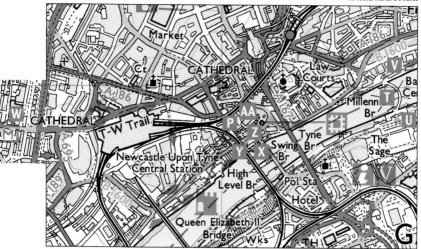

imagine the same sort of scene here a century ago.

Now go around to the other side of the fish market, cross the street near the half-timbered building and turn right. Make a note of where Castle Steps Y are just before you see Bessy Surtees House Z. Read the plaque about Miss Surtees' elopement with John Scott, who later became Lord Eldon, solicitor general, chief justice and lord chancellor. They eloped and got married in Scotland because the Surtees family did not think he was good enough for their daughter. The Surtees' house is an English Heritage property and has rather fine interiors, but leave that until later if you want to complete the quick tour now, having established where it is, and head back to Castle Steps. Go up the steps through the ancient walls of Newcastle, continuing up more steps to the wooden bridge and pass through the Black Gate AA, which was the original entrance to the New Castle P. Cross the road and retrace

your steps to the railway station. With no stopping on the way that's about an hour. The GPS says you've climbed 350 feet (100 metres) altogether, and covered 3.5 miles (5.6 km). A little practice for the more concentrated walking later on.

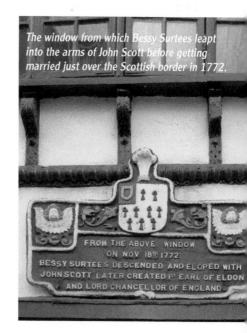

The window from which Bessy Surtees leapt into the arms of John Scott before getting married just over the Scottish border in 1772.

2 Newcastle to St Mary's Lighthouse

via Wallsend, Tynemouth and Whitley Bay

15.2 miles (24.4 km)

As you follow the route described in this book you will come across a wide variety of signs denoting the same route. Be ready to follow the many designations as you go along. You may have noticed a North Sea Trail sign at Newcastle Quayside. This trail encircles the whole of the North Sea. The path covers the North Sea coast of England, Scotland (including Orkney and Shetland), Norway, Sweden, Denmark, Germany, Belgium and France. It is a European designation and later you will see more signs along the route on a blue background as a waymark. Some of the local authorities use the North Sea Trail signage as a regular feature of this route. Others have footpath signs merely saying 'Public Footpath' and others again have their own designations such as Northumberland Coast Path, Berwickshire Coast Path and the John Muir Way.

On this first section of the path today you will see mainly cycleway signs for **Hadrian's Way**, National Route number 72.

Route description

From Newcastle Quayside **A** start walking east downstream, keeping as close to the River Tyne as you can. Pass the Gateshead Millennium Bridge **B** and the river trip boats, continue in front of the houses, still keeping close to the river and turn back on yourself to cross the Ouseburn **C**. Once over this burn you are in Byker. 'Ker' occurs in place names in Celtic-speaking Brittany denoting a defensive settlement or camp. This could refer to pre-Roman camps, which would almost certainly been perched on the hilltop here, or to the mile camp on the Roman wall. This would explain the name of the next settlement you come to on this path: Walker, camp by the wall, and makes sense when the end of the wall is at Wallsend. Old Walker on the maps is right on the Roman wall. Above you, there is a large Victorian red-brick

Hadrian Augustus.

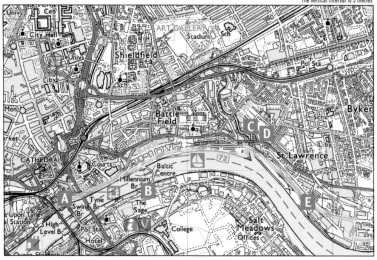

building with pagodas **D**, which the architect intended to resemble a Burmese temple, a place of learning. The building was the Byker School, referred to as the 'Ballast Hills School' by the local kids, because it was built on top of the ballast brought in and dumped here by boats coming to collect coal from Newcastle, such hills sometimes reached considerable heights. You may see more references to 'Ballast Hills' along the Tyne if you read more about the area. The path currently follows the road whilst plans are prepared for the future development of the Riverside, so take St Lawrence Road. Until 2012 there was a large flourmill here, Spillers. The future of Spillers Quay **E** is currently the subject of discussion. The flourmill, when built, was the tallest in Europe and was demolished in 2011.

The road forks and the path is signed to be either side of the building at the fork. The signage you need to follow until you get to Wallsend is the brown

Hadrian's Way signs with an acorn denoting that it is a National Trail.

For the next mile or so you may either follow the Hadrian's Way cycleway, which is the width of a small country lane, traffic free, and has lawns and beautiful wild flowers in the spring and summer or follow the riverside.

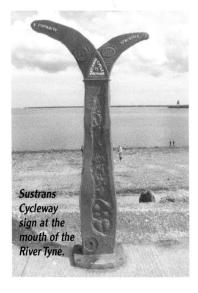

Sustrans Cycleway sign at the mouth of the River Tyne.

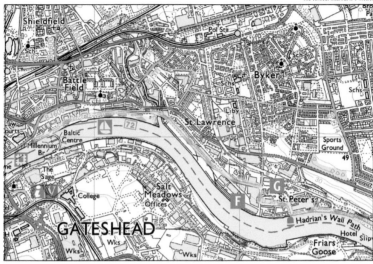

Then the two join, still traffic free, and you are signed all the way to St Mary's Lighthouse. As you near the pedestrian and cycling Tyne Tunnel you'll see cycleway signs for National Route 1 (N). For Chapters 2 and 3 (with the exceptions highlighted in this guide) you'll be following these

The former railway line route is bordered with magnificent wild flowers.

National Route cycleway signs. This guide must be read carefully so that pedestrians can keep off any stretches of road where there is no footway. In the urban areas of Newcastle and North Tyneside, which include some

surprisingly rural stretches and the seafronts at Tynemouth, Cullercoats and Whitley Bay, you'll have no problem in identifying where the path goes once you get used to the variety of signs used. Remember the numbers 72 and 1 (N) apply for the rest of this chapter.

Assuming that you are following the riverside itself, rather than the cycleway, continue along the road. When you have walked the length of the building go around to the back of it. If you have come past the back of the marines depot **F** turn left and then first right into Bottlehouse Street. If you decided on the upper route, turn right down Glasshouse Street and left down Bottlehouse Street. (If you want to follow National Route 72 for flowers, continue straight up St Lawrence Road, pass the St Peter's Wharf new estate **G** and turn left between stone walls which denote access to the cycleway. Turn right along the cycleway and follow the blue no. 72 signs for just under 9 miles (14.5 km).

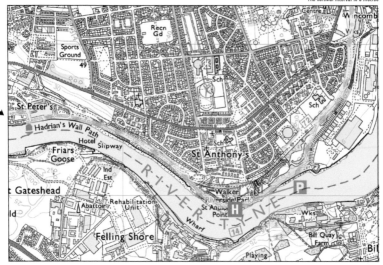

Contours are given in metres
The vertical interval is 5 metres

The Hadrian's Way walkway and cycleway join in the Walker Riverside Park H. If you are in doubt, the cycleway is normally surfaced in black tarmac, about the width of a country lane, and sometimes has a white line down the middle, which is meant to divide pedestrians and cyclists. The cycleway also has a walkway all the way to Lynemouth, as the on-road sections have a normal pavement, which you can safely walk. After Lynemouth (Chapter 3) the cycleway and walkway are normally separate routes and you will start to see signs for 'Northumberland Coast Path'. The signs on that section (Lynemouth to Berwick) are intermittent and you will need this guide and the route descriptions to find your way along it. There are also waymarks with the North Sea Trail symbol – a small wave in blue – along part of the route, however, at the time of writing many were so faded that it is often difficult to see which way they are pointing. It sounds confusing but in practice you will soon get used to the various alternatives. Just make sure you have the route description and the maps in this guide handy at all times.

In any case, assuming you followed the edge of the River Tyne, keep going along the river's edge until the path doubles back on itself and rises to join the cycleway. The long white factory building on the south bank of the river is a specialist marine paintworks. The large blue sheds you will catch a glimpse of are to do with North Sea oil and North Sea energy projects. In fact it would seem that support for

Spillers flour mill, demolished with European funds in 2011.

The once derelict scene on the banks of the Tyne is beginning to come to life with new energy industry linked to the North Sea.

its lawns and woodlands, you will be following the route of the former 'Riverside Branch' of the Byker to Tynemouth Railway all the way to Wallsend, and the Roman camp of Segedunum I.

The Riverside Railway was opened in 1879. The direct Newcastle–North Shields line (now part of the Metro) was a good, fast, route to and from the coast, but was unable to get workers to the new shipyards and other industries which were springing up on the banks of the River Tyne here. The route struggled to get any trade except for the workers. This was because there was the main line to the coast, now

the whole range of major North Sea energy, oil and wind has taken over from shipbuilding on this northern shore of the river.

As you join the main no. 78 cycleway in the Walker Riverside Park H with

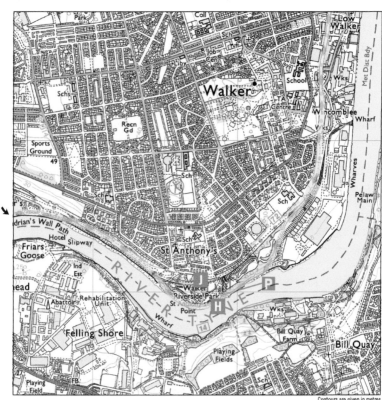

Contours are given in metres
The vertical interval is 5 metres

Contours are given in metres
The vertical interval is 5 metres

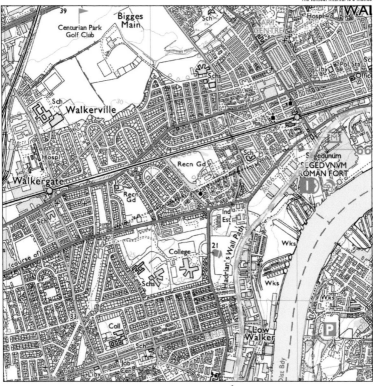

part of the Metro system, and this was faster and more direct for most commuters and shoppers. In addition, from the beginning of the 20th century there was an electric tramway along the nearby main road, now the A186. That was more convenient for nearly everyone who wasn't going to work in the shipyards. To try and attract more trade the operators electrified early, but daytime customers continued to stay away. So finally the trains were scheduled to run only at the beginning and end of the working day – meaning no daylight trains through much of the winter. So staff would turn up to deal with tickets for the early train or trains, and then leave the station until the evening service ran.

The stations were very basic, and by all accounts not very beautiful. Shipbuilding decreased along the Tyne in the second half of the 20th century. Remaining staff began to buy their own cars. Fewer passengers turned up. Byker station (now Morrisons car park) was closed in 1954 and St Anthony's (previously Walker station) in 1960, and the last train to run on the line was in 1973. All the buildings have been demolished, and it now makes a fine traffic-free route for walkers and cyclists.

The path crosses a number of roads, but keep straight on, until there is a fork. Have no fear. Bikes go left, pedestrians right, and you join a

Contours are given in metres
The vertical interval is 5 metres

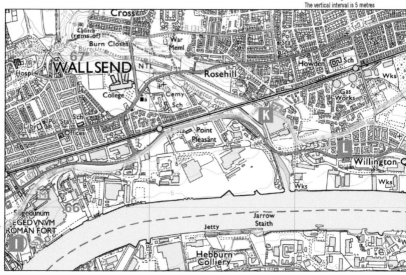

few yards on at the Newcastle city boundary. There is a fine picture of Hadrian on the old bridge abutments here, along with some bicycle wheels, with another North Sea Cycle Route sticker and the acorn/walking man/bicycle Route 72 sign, joined by a Coast to Coast (C2C) sign for good measure. Continue straight across, more or less. Admire the seats for weary walkers, made from sawn-up bridge metals.

Looking south, over the Tyne, you will see a 130-foot (40-metre) high, Victorian spire. This belongs to the former St Andrews Presbyterian Church in Hebburn. There were coal mines in Hebburn, and a major shipyard run by the Leslie family, taken over a few years later by Robert Stephenson and Co. The workers in these enterprises came from all over Britain, and belonged to a range of different churches. The church was designed by the Scottish architect John Johnstone who practised most of his life in Newcastle. He is known for his designs of the French chateau style and a good example of his work is the rather fine Gateshead (Old) Town Hall as well as some other town halls in the area.

The next major feature along the path is the Segedunum I. Here are the remains of the easternmost outpost of Hadrian's Wall, which originally stopped

THIS STONE MARKS THE SOUTH
EASTERN EXTREMITY OF THE
ROMAN WALL WHICH HERE TURNED
SOUTHWARDS TO THE RIVER TYNE.
A ROMAN CAMP BELIEVED TO BE THAT
OF SEGEDUNUM HERE JOINED THE WALL

at Newcastle. You can find out all about that at the museum here (there is an entry fee). It's open all year Monday to Friday in winter and at weekends as well in season (1 April – 31 October). There are also displays relating to the industrial history of Wallsend, a reconstructed Roman bathhouse, a viewing tower to see the whole site and its setting, and a café.

Continue eastwards, past the Carville hand-wash station (a joke, the railway station was called Carville), under the Hadrian's cycleway red steel triumphant archway, and on to a pavement beside the main road. Soon you will see the Hadrian accident repair centre and the Hadrian Lodge Hotel. You are after all on Hadrian Road. Over the tops of houses and down the road towards the river you are looking at the cutting-edge of British technology preparing to exploit wind energy and oil in the North Sea, ready for our future use.

The path stays on the south side of the road until after the next roundabout, after which it crosses to the northern side for about 440 yards (400 metres) before branching left away from the road beside a fine steel railway bridge K which takes the Metro over the valley, through parkland and over the Wallsend Burn. This bears the fine name of Willington Gut before it flows into the Tyne. If you took a riverboat trip whilst at the city Quayside, you may have noticed a tiny port with old fishing boats moored around an inlet by Willington Quay, this is it. Climbing away from the stream, turn right along the pavement on the far side of the road, which cyclists follow.

Just before the prominent Victorian Albion Inn (closed) turn left along the purpose built cycleway signed as route 72 just north of and parallel to the main street of Willington Quay L. There is new housing on your left and industrial units right. After about 300 yards this runs into Armstrong Road, a quiet Edwardian and Victorian Street, virtually traffic free and marked for cycles. Tyneside was and is proud of Armstrong's inventions and achievements (page 33). Most of the local labour force was involved in engineering and the Willington Quay firm of Clelands was building ships, right up until the 1970's. At the end of Armstrong Road there are newer houses. There go left, right and left in quick succession.'

After a very short distance there are pedestrian traffic lights and a sign right (72 E). Follow the trackway. An iron bridge M takes you over the approach roads to the Tyne Tunnel. You can see the Metro line to your north. The white loudhailer-esque structures to the south are the ventilation outlets for the Tyne Tunnel. This path will come down to the main road again where you follow the signs left for Tynemouth which is now 3½ miles (5 km).

Cross the end of the small road and join a dual carriageway, which has a wide strip separate from the road for walkers and cyclists. You come to Royal Quays N and will cross the road following the signs for Shields Ferry (1½ miles) North Shields, Fish Quay, and Tynemouth. You will also pass the junction with the Reivers Cycle Route. More about Reivers later. The route now

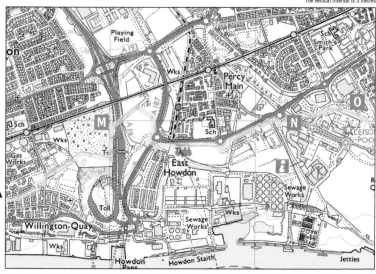

Contours are given in metres
The vertical interval is 5 metres

enters Redburn Dene O, a park with extensive landscaping and artworks alongside the path. Great efforts have been made here to create a pleasant environment, things are looking up, and walking alongside the main road is over. Go downhill towards the river.

Cross the road and bear right, still following the signs for Fish Quay. You will now start to see signs for Whitley Bay, St Mary's Lighthouse and Blyth. Start to follow the signs for Route 1 (N). The path comes down past wooden sleepers inscribed 'Albert Edward Dock'

North Shields Fish Quay.

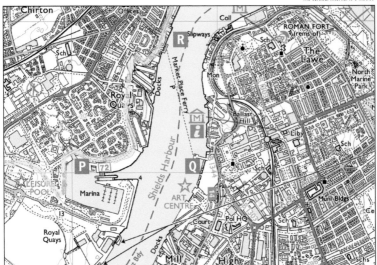

and you arrive at a quayside, a marina and a fishing boat repair yard **P**, with the cycleway and walkway running along a wall in front of some new houses.

The North Sea ferry can be seen behind. Turn left when you arrive at the quayside and go around the back of the boat repair yard **P** until you come out on another road. You will be able to see the landing stage at South Shields for the ferry, which crosses the Tyne at this point. By the time you read this there should be a road and pavement to follow straight through to New Quay **R**. The fine gabled building here is now an architect's office, until recently it was a lively and entertaining music venue. Now follow the sign to the Fish Quay **S**.

Just follow the road east, parallel with the river. It is also signed for the Priory, Castle and Clifford's Fort. There are several information points giving the history of this corner. There is also a blue plaque about the sailors'

home built in the mid-19th century to accommodate 80 visiting seamen.

There are some renovated 19th-century riverside buildings around here, which have been converted into flats. They are good examples of how the area would have looked over 100 years ago, before it became the slums, which you can see in the photos posted on the signs.

The Fish Quay is interesting if you have looked at the Fish Quay in Newcastle because it is still active. Imagine the site in Newcastle, with the fishermen unloading their catches, local people buying them and loading their carts, and the fish shops around the area selling fresh fish from the North Sea. All these things still exist here, as well as a number of fish and chip shops as befits our century. There are also some pubs and restaurants.

Continue around behind the Fish Quay, noting the smokeries on your left as you go towards the Collingwood statue T. Follow the promenade towards the sea. Keep an eye open for the seals, which can be seen these days in the mouth of the River Tyne. There is a sign telling you all about the history of Admiral Collingwood, as well as one about the Tynemouth Volunteer Life Brigade.

The Tynemouth Watch House U was built in 1866 and is now a museum. It is well worth a visit. It is staffed by volunteers and has relatively short opening hours, so make a note to come back if it is not open as you walk past.

As far as following the path to St Mary's Lighthouse is concerned, just follow the promenade from Tynemouth. Tynemouth Village, by the castle, has some very pleasant hostelries and accommodation in the square. There are signs around the square stating that stag and hen parties are not welcome in the village. Perhaps you might get a quieter night's sleep here than further along the seafront, although there is excellent accommodation in Cullercoats Y and Whitley Bay as well. The main features to look out for along the front are well signed and attractive as well as interesting. After the museum of the Tynemouth Volunteer Life Brigade, there is the mediaeval Tynemouth Castle and Priory W. There you can see not only the ruins of the mediaeval

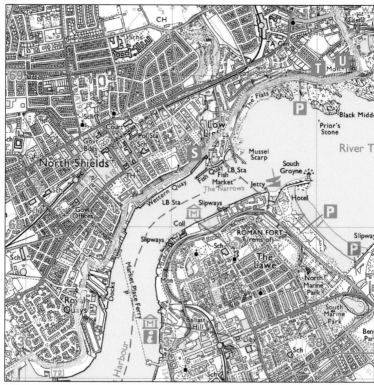

Contours are given in metres
The vertical interval is 5 metres

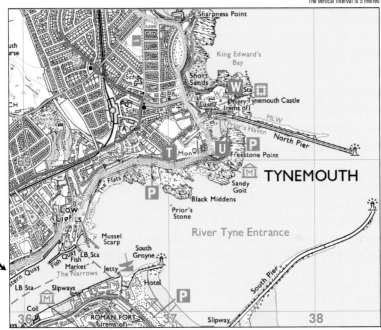

Contours are given in metres
The vertical interval is 5 metres

Sharpness Point

King Edward's
Bay

Short
Sands

Priory Tynemouth Castle
Castle (rems of)

MLW

Prior's Haven

North Pier

Freestone Point

TYNEMOUTH

The Flats

Sandy
Goit

Black Middens

Prior's
Stone

River Tyne Entrance

Mussel
Scarp

Low
Lights

South
Groyne

Fish Quay Fish
Market
The Narrows

Jetty

Hotel

South Pier

LB Sta

Slipways

Coll

ROMAN FORT
(rems of)

Slipway

36

37

38

buildings but also Second World War gun emplacements which have been recreated to look and sound as they did during that time. Amongst the ruins of the priory is a beautiful chapel, and in the red brick house is an exhibition about the history of this headland.

Newcastle to St Mary's Lighthouse

The Tynemouth Watch House was built in 1866 and is now a museum. It is well worth a visit.

The spectacular ruins of a fine mediaeval priory at Tynemouth.

Cullercoats **Y** is famous for the artist colony there during the 19th century. If you visited the Laing Art Gallery in Newcastle you will already be familiar with their work and can now enjoy the scenery that they painted. You will also have a clear idea of how the area would have looked 150 years ago. Many of the buildings which you will see along the front, and which feature in their pictures, are still there. They have blue plaques and information signs which make interesting reading.

Next is St Matthew's Church **X** with its fine spire. There you can read about the architect and the other famous buildings with which he is associated. The Dove Marine Laboratory of Newcastle University is famous for its research on all things marine and its association with the lifeboat stations here is also fascinating. The Cullercoats Fisherman's Lookout has an interesting history. The fishermen's families had to go out onto the open cliffs during fog and stormy weather to keep watch and

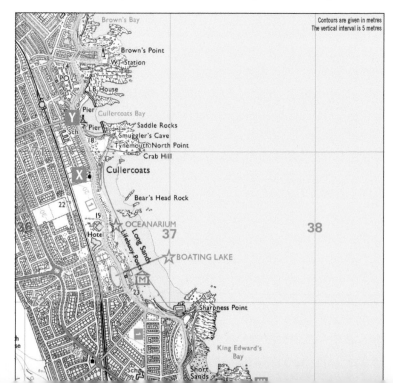

Cullercoats fisherman's lookout.

help the fishermen in. This building was constructed to give a good view and a place away from the raw elements to do so.

Spanish City **Z**, the place with the white dome, was built in 1912 and was a major attraction, which led Whitley Bay to be nicknamed the 'Blackpool of the North East'. There are plans to bring it back to its former glory and play a role in Whitley Bay's future as a popular resort.

The Spanish City.

Contours are given in metres
The vertical interval is 5 metres

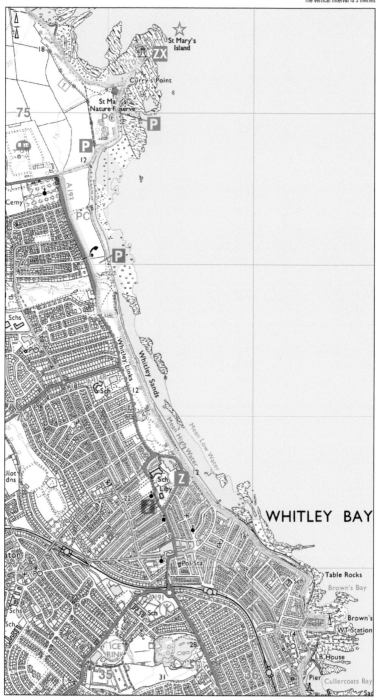

St Mary's Island

ZX

Curry's Point

St Mary's
Nature Reserve

PC

P

P

A193

Cemy

PC

P

Whitley Links

Whitley Sands

Schs

PO

Sch

Mean High Water

Mean Low Water

Sch
Liby

Z

WHITLEY BAY

Allot
Gdns

Sch

Pol Sta

Sch

Table Rocks

Brown's Bay

aton

PO

Brown's
W T Station

Schs

Sch

Sch

PO

L B House

ICE
RINK

35

31

36

Pier

Cullercoats Bay

Sad

St Mary's Lighthouse.

As you walk along the front there are all sorts of little curiosities which may catch your eye. Finishing up at St Mary's Lighthouse **ZX** will make a pleasant end to this section of the walk. I hope you agree that the overall experience of walking from the centre of Newcastle to this point on the Northumberland coast has been as interesting and rewarding as I found it when researching this book.

3 St Mary's Lighthouse to Newbiggin-by-the-Sea

via Blyth and Bedlington

16.3 miles (26.6 km)

The path for the next 16 miles (25 km) crosses or circumvents several river estuaries. As well as industrial archaeological interest there may be wading birds on the mud flats, seals on the sandy beaches, flowers in the dunes and dramatic red sandstone cliffs. A few years ago it was all coal mines, factories, smoke and grime. That's all changed now and you join the National Cycle Route, and local roads (both have footways) to get you through this section.

From St Mary's Lighthouse **A** the cycleway starts off well back from the cliff at the landward side of the car park. For walkers there is a path just back from the cliff, which takes you towards Hartley Bay **B** and Seaton Sluice **C**. The path is narrow but well surfaced. When you see a row of 1930s houses on your left follow the path through to the road and turn right onto the pavement, which is on the landward side of the road. Go north towards Seaton Sluice. Here you can explore the headland by following the lawn above the sea wall. At the far side of the headland you can see the actual sluice. This was constructed as an additional access directly from the sea to the beautiful little harbour, the mouth of the Seaton Brook.

Seaton Sluice is a quiet place to walk and Seaton Delaval Hall is just a short walk up the road inland.

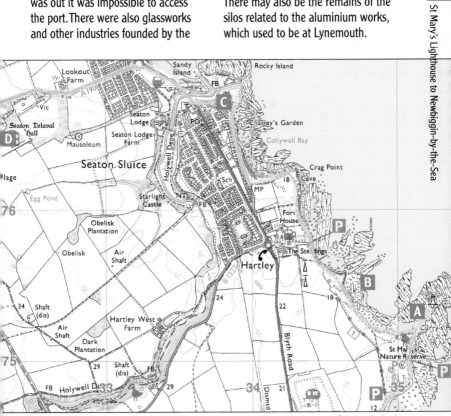

The chimneys of the former aluminium smelter at Lynemouth, and wind generators.

The sluice is a rock-cut channel like a mini Corinth Canal designed to increase the capacity of the tiny port behind it. There was a colliery here at Hartley with an output greater than the original and current access – which you can see at the end of the beach – could handle, because when the tide was out it was impossible to access the port. There were also glassworks and other industries founded by the owners of Seaton Delaval Hall **D**. There are signs telling you all about this as well as a couple of pubs and some accommodation here. The scene is generally attractive.

Look across the bay and you'll see the wind turbines around Blyth ahead. There may also be the remains of the silos related to the aluminium works, which used to be at Lynemouth.

Contours are given in metres
The vertical interval is 5 metres

Before going on along the coast I would highly recommend a visit to Seaton Delaval Hall D. It is a ten-minute walk inland up the road and is owned by the National Trust. It was designed by the architect and playwright John Vanbrugh, he of the naughty restoration plays. The displays in the hall describe the unusual way of life of the family there. They also explain how the hall came to be burned down, and to this day largely remains a shell. It is well worth a visit nevertheless.

Having visited Seaton Delaval Hall return to Seaton Sluice and cross the bridge. There is a well-surfaced path leading through the dunes all the way to the outskirts of Blyth. The path is called the Eve Black Coastal Walkway

E. You can also go the whole way on the beach if you're happy to scramble around the breakwaters. The beach walk will be quieter as the dunes are rather close to the road and traffic noise is definitely audible. Be warned that it is best to keep a wide birth of any seals on the beach.

As you come into Blyth you'll see the enormous yellow storage shed F of the Port of Blyth. Just south of this are some steps and the bandstand. You will have passed a number of wartime installations, as well as the cemetery on the landward side of the road.

Either join the main road just beyond the bandstand, or take the footpath leading onto the road through the

dunes just before the Port of Blyth storage facility **F**. There are some explanatory signs about the wartime installations. In both world wars Blyth was a submarine harbour and had to be strongly defended. It was also an important shipbuilding port and built the First World War *Ark Royal* naval ship.

Having joined the main road, walk north along the pavement for a short distance before turning right into the park **G**. The park was given to the people of Blyth by the Ridley family.

Their family seat is upstream at Blagdon Hall.

The Ridleys had coal on their land, and still do, and were leading members of the Newcastle scene through the centuries. They held senior positions in Newcastle and in the county of Northumberland and you may remember reading some of their memorials in Newcastle Cathedral. Two members of the family are particularly remembered for playing a part on the national stage. Bishop Nicholas Ridley was cruelly burnt at the stake for his

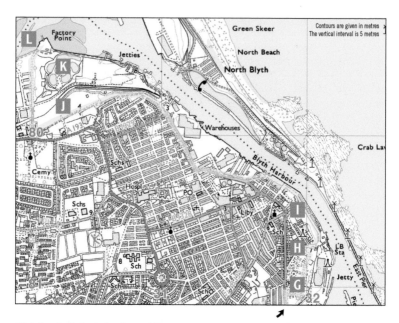

Contours are given in metres
The vertical interval is 5 metres

Christian beliefs at the time of Queen Mary. Nicholas Ridley, the government minister, will be remembered for his efforts to negotiate a peaceful solution to the Falklands/Malvinas sovereignty dispute in the late 20th century. Events overtook his hard work and put the clock back for another generation.

There is a lively scene at Ridley Park G. It's popular with families and there is a small café. Make for the coastal end of the park and exit next to the War Memorial H. Keep on down the road towards the harbour and turn left along the harbourside. You will see an ancient lighthouse on your left. The Spirit of the Staithes I is a work of art on the harbour's edge. Continue along the harbour's edge through some interesting blue iron gates. Signs will direct you to the left of the buildings facing you. For the time being, follow the cycleway signs for Bedlington. It is also signed 'Coast and Castles 1 North' or 'C&C 1 (N)'. Plessey is the name of a local village, in

case you are wondering about the origin of any street names round here.

The path/cycleway will take you back to the streets of Blyth on the roads nearest to the river. So take a right briefly on to the A193 and, after 100 yards (91 metres), just before a garage on the corner, turn right, then first left, past Morpeth Road Primary School J, which has a pit wheel in the playground. Keep straight on past the traffic barriers and then take a sharp right past a barrier pole – which stops cars going through – down the long straight road, which takes you directly to the coast.

On your right you will see some signs explaining how the water coming out of the mines nearby is badly polluted and has to be purified before going back into the sea. You can walk through this area of ponds K if you like, turning left down a gravel track to rejoin the coast path just before it meets the estuary.

The path follows the estuary inland along the edge of the River Blyth Estuary L for 1½ miles (2 km). The power stations on the far side of the estuary are now closed but the electricity pylons remain. In other parts of the country such sites are now being used as points where electricity generated from turbines out at sea is brought in, and one can well imagine that this may be the case here in the future.

In the River Blyth Estuary here there are moored small colourful leisure boats and numbers of herons and redshanks, along with oystercatchers, ringed plovers and a host of other wading birds. The path, soon signed for 'Bedlington via Riverside' and Ashington is now going to follow the estuary upstream as far as Furness Bridge M. At one point where the cycleway continues along the road, a wooden bridleway sign 'Public

Bridleway Furnace Bridge' leads you out to a the headland N and across a field or two where horses graze, enabling you to get away from the road. This bridleway rejoins the cycleway, which continues more or less all the way along the edge of the Blyth Estuary to Furness Bridge.

At Furness Bridge there was a corn mill until 1759, when it was taken over and replaced by a blast furnace, taking advantage of the coal and iron nodules in the local rock, then abundant here on the banks of the river. By 1819 Michael Longridge was in charge. To get cheaper coal from Choppington coal mine, 2 miles away, he planned to install a wagonway between here and the coal mine. He had read a report by Robert Stevenson (note the 'v') of Edinburgh, now mainly known as the Scottish lighthouse designer, who put forward the idea that wrought or malleable

The Spirit of the Staithes.

iron would be better than cast iron for rails. His agent, George Birkinshaw, took out a patent on the idea and the ironworks here started producing the rails. George Stephenson had just been asked to build the Stockton and Darlington Railway and adapted the new rail design after he had inspected the innovative 2-mile (3.2-km) wagonway at Furness Bridge. The production of rails here was massive in comparison with any previous similar enterprise and the rails were exported worldwide. Following this success the first locomotive, the *Michael Longridge* was built here in 1837. The first passenger train ever to leave London King's Cross was hauled by a Bedlington Locomotive, as were the first trains in Italy and Holland.

The works closed down in 1867 as production picked up elsewhere, and in 1959 the derelict buildings were demolished and the area renamed Dene Park. Now it's a peaceful Bedlington Country Park M.

From Furness Bridge cross the river following signs for Bedlington Station and turn right up the road for a short distance. The cycleway/walkway branches off right, parallel with the river, goes under a railway line, and turns left, parallel with the railway line, and away from the river along a quiet road with Bedlingtonshire Community High School O alongside it.

Bedlingtonshire consisted of the parish of Bedlington only, an exclave,

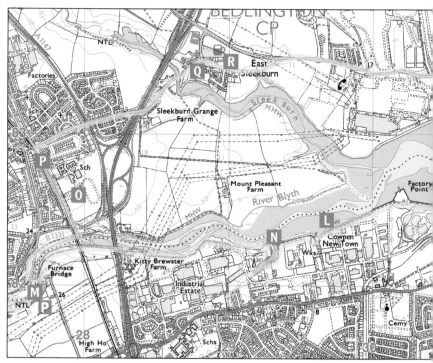

Contours are given in metres
The vertical interval is 5 metres

or detached part, of County Durham. Until quite recently these detached villages were in quite a few places around England and Wales. In 1844 Bedlington was transferred to the county of Northumberland, but the name, and the tradition, leads to names like that of the school.

You arrive at Bedlington Station P, a settlement near Bedlington, which no longer has a station. When you reach a busy street on a sharp corner turn right, following the cycle path signs and following the pavement, keeping straight on at any junctions. The path and road rises over a bridge crossing the A189, then crosses the Sleek Burn, and comes into the village called East Sleek Burn. Where the cycleway turns sharp left in front of a bungalow Q do **not** follow the cycleway. Keep straight on past a public house, the General Havelock R, and follow the disused road for about a third of a mile (0.5 km). The road here has a safe pedestrian pavement and you can follow it to Cambois, pronounced 'Kemiss'.

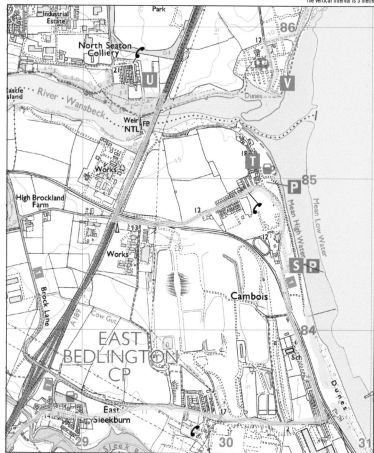

When you reach the coast turn left along the pavement, past the local camera club and Cambois Miners' Welfare Institute S, and past a former coal mine marked by some of its machinery, or go onto and follow the beach northwards. This is one of the many quiet beaches you will come across along this coastline.

Before you reach the River Wansbeck, which gives the district its name, there is a recess in the dunes and a pub T. The next great obstacle is the River

Wansbeck, but here a well surfaced and maintained cycleway/footway goes alongside the A189, which is a bit noisy but achieves the crossing safely and quickly. Future plans envisage a riverside path from this point. However, at the time of writing, you follow the pavement inland alongside the road, cross the railway, join the cycleway alongside the A186 and go north to cross the river Wansbeck.

As soon as you have crossed the river, look out for a small gap in the hedge with the cycleway sign on the top of the bank . Go left (north) through the gap and along the track. You are on the outskirts of North Seaton Colliery, which no longer has a colliery. Go for 20 or 30 yards upstream and you will see a flight of steps to the left towards a weir. Go down the steps and to the river's edge. Turn downstream on the public footpath and make your way through the dunes. Fork left where the path divides but go to the top of the riverbank  before reaching the open sea.

When I visited this area campers were making their way along the cliff top to Newbiggin-by-the-Sea to spend their money in the hostelries and eating places of that seaside resort which is about a mile away. The path was well trodden and I'm sure that Newbiggin-by-the-Sea could do with their holiday spending money, as well as yours. There were however signs put up by the county council warning of cliff danger and stating that the official path is closed. I have been assured that the county council has the matter in hand and the path should be officially open by the time you read this. At other points along this path such problems have evidently been dealt with very swiftly by the county council and I am confident that this will be the case by the time you arrive here. (Should the path really be blocked then you can follow a public bridleway, which follows the main camp entrance road. At that point you may wish to join the cycleway and bypass Newbiggin, following the cycleway signs to Lynemouth, and then following the instructions in this book which take you through Ellington and down to Cresswell.) Another alternative is to follow the cycleway towards Ashington

Newbiggin-by-the-Sea with its brand new sandy beach.

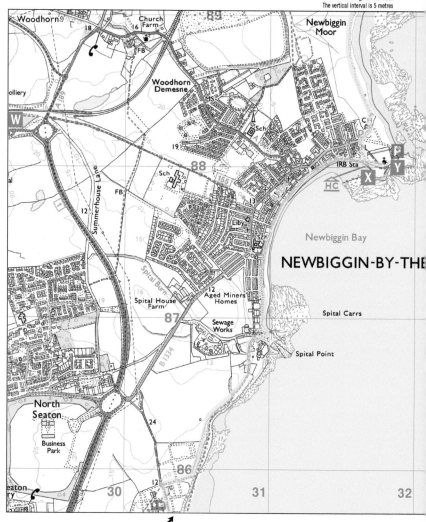

Contours are given in metres
The vertical interval is 5 metres

and stay there for the night, and then retrace your steps to the Queen Elizabeth Country Park where you can visit the Woodhorn Museum **W**, which is an absolute must in any case at some stage of this part of your visit.

Assuming that the path is open continue along the cliff top to Newbiggin-by-the-Sea, make for the promenade as soon as you can see it beneath you and continue

towards Church Point, with its steepled church. You will find the people of Newbiggin friendly and helpful. There is accommodation here and some shops and cafés. The Maritime Centre **X** has displays that explain the history of the place extremely well, and you will get a good picture of the past of this area.

On the beach, which has beautiful golden sand, a coal seam emerges right by the village, and is exploited

A coal seam emerging in the beach is exploited daily.

on a daily basis whilst the tide is out. A 36-ton lorry comes to collect the coal dust, which is extracted here on a regular basis. This dust, called dross, is taken south to provide energy for industry. In the bay stands a sculpture, 'the Couple'. I believe they are locally called Ebb and Flo, a little joke about the tides that swirled around them, rather than the idea that Ebenezer and Florence are their names. To find out more about the Couple and a series of the artworks around visit the Newbiggin Maritime Centre X. Here there is also a café and lots of other information. The church Y is well worth a visit. You have to enquire about opening times when volunteers will be there to welcome you.

WOODHORN MUSEUM

To make sense of the recent history of the walk described so far, and likewise the scenery which makes up the major features of Chapter 4, I would highly recommend a visit to the Woodhorn Colliery Museum. Where coal mines used to stand with their Victorian villages, railway lines, spoil heaps and all the trappings of the industrial age, are now green fields, large lakes, nature reserves and a coast path. A viewing of how it was just a few decades ago – as shown in this museum – will greatly enrich your visit, and enable you to understand

how the locals feel as you may meet them along the way on the path or in the pubs.

To make your way to the Woodhorn Museum return along the promenade and find the cycleway which leads all the way to the Museum, National Route 155. The museum is marked on the maps as Woodhorn Colliery. When you first arrive at the colliery you may feel the site is a bit deserted. Do not expect the sort of lively scene you might find at the Beamish Museum in County Durham, with lively young ex-miners explaining every aspect of life in the colliery village in the 20th

Ebb and Flo.

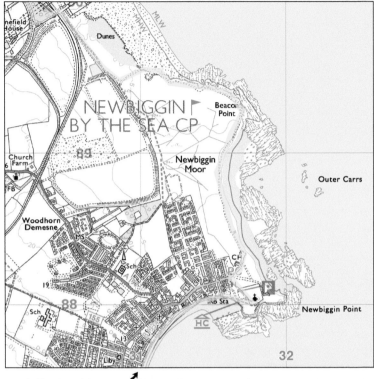

Dramatic wave forms around Newbiggin during relatively calm weather are said to be the result of water-filled cavities, produced by mining under the bay.

The wonderful Woodhorn Colliery Museum can be reached on foot from Newbiggin or Ashington, following the cycleways.

century. Nevertheless, the buildings are still here and this is (I believe) the only colliery still standing in Northumberland. There is an excellent exhibition showing how this area would have looked until the 1980s. As you go north from Newbiggin across Druridge Bay and into Amble you will be able to imagine how this whole area would have looked when coal mining was in its prime. Having visited the area since the 1960s I find it hard to believe that the beautiful countryside over the next 20 miles or so was once a grim industrial scene with coal tips and mines, smoke, grime, and quite a lot of poverty and dereliction along the way. Now there are nature reserves, lakes frequented by migrating birds, paths bordered by beautiful wild flowers,

and sandy beaches for many miles. A visit to Woodhorn Museum will be a revelation and help you to imagine how this area once was.

During the walk covered by this chapter you may have sometimes wondered what on earth you were doing wandering along through some scenes of neglect and desertion. Hopefully when you complete the walk you will see that it is a glimpse of the transition that most people in other parts of Britain do not know exists and it should give you a real understanding of this corner of England.

In the next chapter I will describe how to progress along the coast on foot and, on separate pavements, to Warkworth.

4 Newbiggin-by-the-Sea to Warkworth

via Lynemouth and Amble

16 miles (26 km)

For the next 60 or so miles (96 km) the Northumberland coast can be followed more or less within sight and sound of the sea. In many places you can choose to walk along the sandy beaches, or choose the path in or just behind the dunes, where the floral displays can be stunning in spring and summer. You will have the opportunity to view at close range, again best in spring and summer, Coquet Island (no landing), Inner Farne, Staple and Longstone islands. The National Trust, RSPB, Northumberland Wildlife Trust and Natural England have managed these islands, and a number of other nature reserves, as safe havens to ensure that some of the rarest plants and birds of Britain are not only thriving, but are open as far as possible to you, the visitor. Along with the fishermen who take their lobster pots off their boats, stack them attractively on the harbourside, and install seats and life-saving equipment, these organisations work hard to present all of this. The trips will cost, but you will not regret the investment. In this and later chapters this guide will help you to decide which trips to take. They are all quite different, and careful choices will be required according to your interests and time available.

To continue north from Newbiggin-by-the-Sea go to the bus stop at the end of the road. Go between the golf club and the caravan site **A**, along the track, which continues along the cliff top to Beacon Point **B** and onwards towards Lynemouth Power Station **C** through the dunes. You should be able to do this without going on to the golf course itself. There may be places where you have to walk along the edge of the lawns. In case you're worried that this part of the route is not marked as a public footpath, I have it on the authority of a number of locals that they have walked this route for over 60 years. The golfers here are friendly, they have an excellent golf course, and the local councils are happy for you to walk this route. At the far north end of the golf course there is a lawn covered in rabbit holes and at this point it will be best to go to the far north-west corner of the area where you will join the marked public footpath.

As you approach the power station keep close to the fence on the inland side of the dune area and look out for three 'dragon's teeth', the giant cubes of concrete which were installed along this coast to deter the enemy in

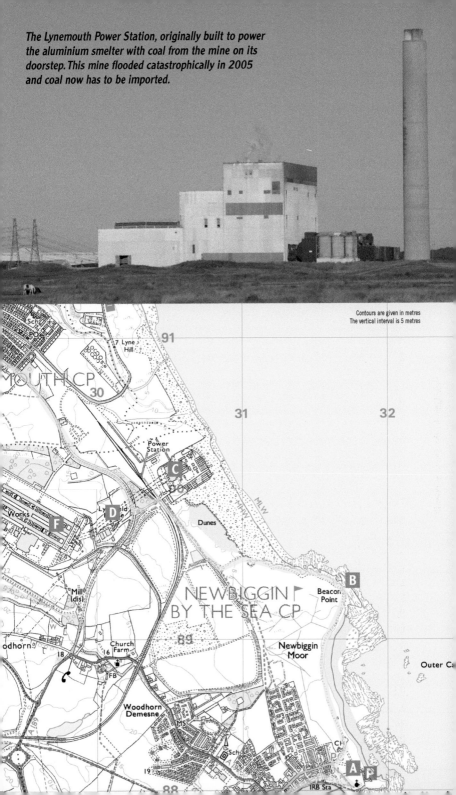

The Lynemouth Power Station, originally built to power the aluminium smelter with coal from the mine on its doorstep. This mine flooded catastrophically in 2005 and coal now has to be imported.

The Lynemouth Aluminium Smelter was opened in 1974.

the Second World War. Between the dragon's teeth and the fence there is a small gap. Squeeze through and you will find a signed and railed path. The yellow rails are there to protect you from any heavy machinery coming out of the storage area above. The sign says 'Public Footpath to Newbiggin'. Cross the main access road of the power station and you'll find an off-road cleway/walkway, which takes you to the main road. Now cross the main

road D, turn right onto the path and this will take you into Lynemouth E.

The Lynemouth Aluminium Smelter F was opened in 1974 and closed in March 2012 with the loss of several hundred jobs. It used an enormous amount of electricity and the reason for choosing this site was the availability of the coal. At the time this enabled the power station to be totally fuelled from local coal. Another point in favour

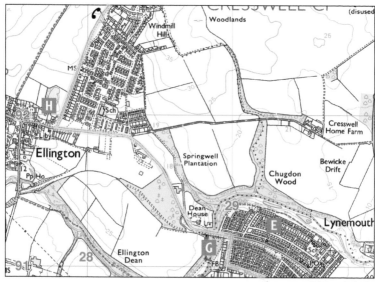

Contours are given in metres
The vertical interval is 5 metres

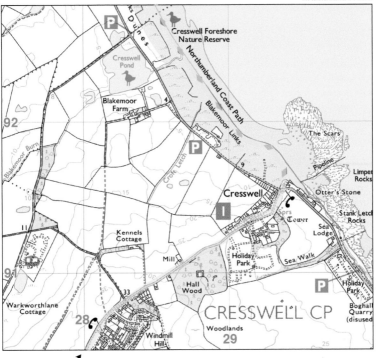

of this site was the proximity of a port (Blyth), which can take relatively large ships, the existing railway system, and a large pool of ex-miners used to challenging work.

The power station was completed in 1972 right next to the output point of Ellington and Lynemouth collieries. It used over one million tons of coal every year and 3,000 people were employed at the two collieries at that time, with over half their output going to the power station. From 1994 the two collieries were connected by an underground passage and the coal was brought by conveyor belts all the way to the power station. However, the Ellington Colliery had to be closed after a catastrophic flooding of the galleries in 2005. Initially the power station used up current stocks, then it was supplied by open-cast mines in the area, finally most of the coal had to be imported. Alternative forms of fuel have been tried. It is intended that the power station should continue to serve the locality and the National Grid. The aluminum smelting works is being found alternative uses, primarily as an industrial estate.

As you come into Lynemouth go straight ahead along the street you are in as far as you can go. At the westernmost end of Park Road G turn right into Fenham Road. At the end of this road turn left for a 15-minute walk into Ellington. At the first main junction H turn right into Ellington (you can cross the lawns here), follow signs for Cresswell, keep walking on the pavement of Cresswell Road for 2 miles (3 km).

At Cresswell I you'll start seeing signs for the Northumberland Coast Path. Look back to see the first of many pele towers (the spelling varies, and I will give an account of them later). The path now takes to the beach. Only at the very highest tides and in the worst weather will this be difficult. The road here is very quiet and could be followed in this case, but it would be better to check tides ahead of your journey and have a nice wide beach to walk along.

After 1.5 miles (2 km) keep an eye on the dunes and look for a gap with a scattering of dragon's teeth on the beach J and a very substantial Second World War concrete structure back in the dunes. Turn left at this building, there is a path here, which takes you on to some National Trust land and the track giving access to the parking area.

Continue north for a short distance and you'll see a path going inland about 600 yards (550 metres) from the car park entrance. This path leads to Low Chibburn Preceptory K. If you have an interest in the Middle Ages you may find this isolated building quite interesting. The ruins of the chapel there are the remains of a group of buildings installed by the Knights Hospitallers. This organisation, which was quite separate from the Knights Templar though they had similar aims, had both military and religious branches. There is little in the written records to indicate the exact use of this building, but we can assume that it is on the route of pilgrims going to Lindisfarne in the Middle Ages and that it would have

been staffed at the expense of the Knights Hospitallers, who received donations from wealthy people who were worried about going to heaven when they died. In the Middle East you can see their magnificent fortified Crusader castles, here is a tiny example of their work back in their home country. The establishment would almost certainly have had to be defended, giving a role to their military wing as well.

The buildings adjoining it, which until the 20th century had earthwork surrounding, are called the Dower House, and would have been built after Henry VIII had the religious establishment closed down and handed the property over to a local landowner. There are signs exploring more of the history on site. Return to the Coast Path and turn left. For the next 5 miles (8 km) you just keep going along the path behind the dunes to Amble and 2 miles (3 km) along the track is Ladyburn Lake L, surrounded by the Druridge Bay Country Park. In school holidays and summer weekends the Country Park Centre may be open. There is a café there, some local information and some books for sale.

This site was proposed as being suitable for a nuclear power station at one point, but a country park seems to have won the day. If you read signs erected by protestors against wind power along the inland route of the official Northumberland Coast Path north of Belford, you will see that they support nuclear power by preference. So there is the choice.

Contours are given in metres
The vertical interval is 5 metres

VINGTON
CP

East Chevington
Nature reserve

Hadston Links

Chibburn
Mouth

Chibburn
Links

Druridge Bay

Druridge Bay
Nature Reserve

Chapel
(remains of)

K

Low Chibburn
(remains of)

High
Chibburn

Druridge
Links

J

Stonecroft

Druridge

Hemscott
Hill

Mean High Water

Mean Low Water

Hemscotthill Links

TON
CP

P

29

Cresswell Foreshore

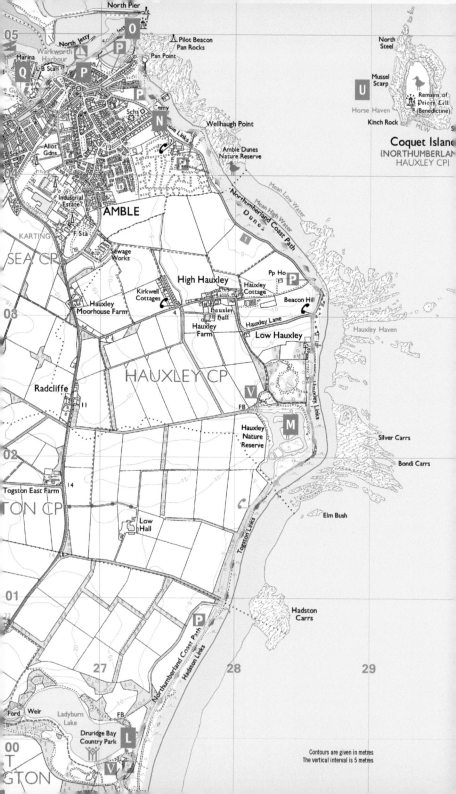

North Pier

North Jetty
South Jetty

O

Pilot Beacon
Pan Rocks

Pan Point

05

Warkworth
Harbour
Marina
L-B Stn

Q

P

P

P

Schs

P

N

Academy

Wellhaugh Point

Amble Dunes
Nature Reserve

F

Allot
Gdns

04

Industrial
Estate

AMBLE

Northumberland Coast Path

Mean High Water

Mean Low Water

D u n e s

KARTING

SEA CP

F. Sta

Sewage
Works

Pp Ho

P

03

Kirkwell
Cottages

High Hauxley

Hauxley
Cottage

Beacon Hill

Hauxley
Moorhouse Farm

Hauxley
Hall

Hauxley Lane

Hauxley
Farm

Low Hauxley

Hauxley Haven

HAUXLEY CP

Radcliffe

V

FB

M

Hauxley
Nature
Reserve

Hauxley Links

02

Silver Carrs

Bondi Carrs

Togston East Farm

TON CP

Low
Hall

Elm Bush

Togston Links

01

Hadston
Carrs

P

Northumberland Coast Path

Hadston Links

27

28

29

Ford
Weir

Ladyburn
Lake

FB

Druridge Bay
Country Park

L

00

TOGSTON

V

North
Steel

Mussel
Scarp

U

Horse Haven

Remains of
Priory Cell
(Benedictine)

Kinch Rock

MLW

Coquet Island

(NORTHUMBERLAND
HAUXLEY CP)

Contours are given in metres
The vertical interval is 5 metres

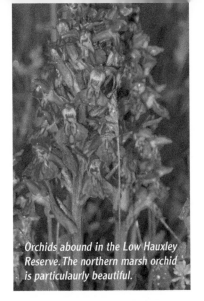

Orchids abound in the Low Hauxley Reserve. The northern marsh orchid is particulaurly beautiful.

Continue another 2 miles (3 km) and you'll see the entrance gate to the Northumberland Wildlife Trust's wonderful Low Hauxley Nature Reserve M. In winter this will be worth a visit to see the wintering wildfowl from the hides. In spring and summer take a short walk inland to the visitor centre, which is often staffed by voluntary wardens. They keep up-to-date records on whiteboards, can explain the flowers and birds and answer queries on any plants, animals or birds, which you may not be sure about. This is a beautiful reserve with excellent service. Make sure you leave time for some exploring here. From the Low Hauxley reserve to the harbourside at Amble it is now only 2 miles (3 km). You can walk along parts of the beach here, or stay on the

path over Hauxley Links, along a short stretch of quiet road. Continue onwards through the dunes as far as the cemetery with its obelisk N, which you will see from quite a distance. Keep to the landward side of the houses on the far side of the cemetery. Cross the lawns to the seaward side of all the houses. If the tide is low enough and the sea not too stormy, you can follow the official Coast Path route onto the south jetty. Turn left at the end of the first section of jetty O and keep going down South Jetty to Amble harbour.

Amble has accommodation, is a fishing harbour, and has boat trips in spring to see the puffins, roseate and other terns on Coquet Island. There are cafés, pubs and real shops in the town, as well as a launderette and chip shops.

On the harbour P you'll see boards advertising the boat trips out to Coquet Island U or you can make enquiries at the tourist information centre. The skipper of the boat I took also maintains the Coquet Island lighthouse and had many entertaining stories of the trials and tribulations of that work. It was a very good morning's entertainment, and the birdwatching was excellent. The need to protect the wildlife on this island is paramount, and no landing is allowed by casual

Coquet Island. There is no landing, but you get a pretty good view of the puffins and rare roseate terns from the boats that go from Amble Harbour in the spring and early summer.

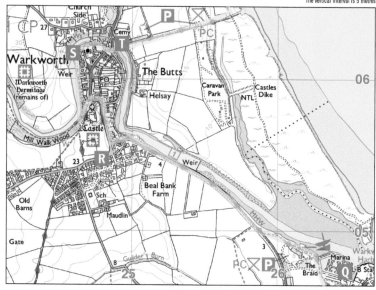

visitors. However, if the weather is good, you will get a trip around the island. If it's a bit windy then the boat will go as close as it can to the puffin and tern nesting areas and you will get a very good view.

Until the late 20th century Amble was a coal port and mining town. Now it has caravan sites and a marina, and fishermen have returned to the harbour, making quite an attractive

scene. As you come away from the harbour's edge at its western corner go down the road for a short distance, turn right through a car park and then left out of the car park and the path is clearly marked to the landward side of the marina Q. It joins the main road to Warkworth and you follow the pavement alongside the River Coquet. There will be swans, eider ducks, herons and a number of waders, the latter especially at low tide. As you come into

Warkworth Castle.

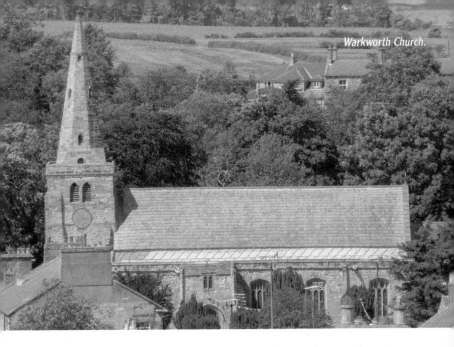

Warkworth Church.

Warkworth the road rises and you come to a junction. Turn right towards the magnificent Warkworth Castle **R**.

Every castle you will see along this route is quite different. I would say that every castle is worth visiting, each one with its own extraordinary history, each one with a completely different appearance. Warkworth Castle is quite different from the New Castle at Newcastle. It has chambers, which are still vaulted, a good view of the surrounding countryside, and no railway lines or railway stations built across it. It's great to explore inside. There are signs showing how it would have looked when occupied. You will be looking at this castle as you go along the coast and it's good to know what it looks like inside as you look back. As an extra bonus Shakespeare makes mention of this mediaeval fortress as the setting for Lady Percy's tragic parting from Harry Hotspur in *Henry IV Part One*, Scene 3. Hotspur's opening speech in this scene is as good a guide as any to the complex, dangerous and uncertain politics of the period when such castles were in full use.

Continuing down the street in Warkworth you come to a left fork, which leads to the village church **S**. In this corner of the village there are several pubs, local shops and a post office.

Go inside the church, which is probably the most complete Norman village church in the county, and inside you will find a fine knight in armour occupying somebody else's plinth, and several periods of mediaeval building to give the church a very pleasing interior.

To continue your walk go down the lane to the left of the church and walk upstream the short distance until you see the castle above the trees reflected in the River Coquet. Then retrace your steps along the river bank to the mediaeval bridge with its guardhouse **T**.

5 Warkworth to Craster

via Alnmouth and Boulmer

13 miles (21 km)

This very pleasant walk takes you from one magnificent, ruined, lordly Northumbrian castle to the next. The walk can start with a loop around the dunes and beach on the seaward side of the Coquet estuary, with fine views of Warkworth Castle, great duneland flowers, and lots of activity to watch as the many various birds fly in and out to feed in the tidal flats here. After that, follow the cycleway into Alnmouth, enjoying the pubs and views if you have time. The path rises to Alnmouth Golf Club and then follows the beach for about half a mile, crosses Seaton Point and arrives in the coastal hamlet of Boulmer with its fishing cobles, the tractors that tow them in and out of the water and the Fishing Boat Inn. Next come some quiet bays and Howick. I recommend a detour to Howick Hall for its gardens and arboretum. Howick Hall is and was home of the earls Grey, of tea fame as well as the parliamentary reform that brought the beginnings of democracy to this country along with a much reduced bill for policing riots. There is a good café but be sure to check opening hours first. Finally, after passing a dramatic kittiwake cliff, we arrive at Craster and its kipper smokeries, the Jolly Fisherman and glimpses ahead all the time of Dunstanburgh Castle.

Cross the mediaeval bridge **A** at the northern end of the village and turn immediately right up a straight quiet road going directly towards the coast. Here the road forks, left for the golf club and right for Coquet Caravan Site. Keep straight on here, past the toilets and keep going towards the sea down to the track going north. If you have time to explore the dunes here you can walk through to the North Pier. You could go along the track behind the dunes as far as the North Pier and return along the beach for a nice round walk if you have time. You'll get good views of Coquet Island and Warkworth

Castle. If you have binoculars you will see herons, swans and waders around the estuary as well as more birds along the shoreline.

Continuing the walk, keep going north behind the dunes. If you are in need of refreshment at this point the golf club **B** welcomes visitors on foot. Many of the golf clubs along the Northumberland coast have a sign welcoming walkers, and I am assured by a number of members that as long as you are reasonably well turned out the golfing dress code posted at the door will not be strictly enforced!

Where the path comes very close to the beach **C** you'll see a valley on your left in the dunes with a bridge crossing it. This is to enable the golfers to get to the far end of the course more easily. The path goes inland here under the bridge. At the top of the hill follow the track going right, past some vehicle barriers or gates until you come to the caravan site entrance **D**. Here the path is marked on maps as going along the inland fence. In fact you follow the track through the caravan site, then left at the junction of the tracks and then straight on. Soon you cross a stream over a wooden bridge and come to a National Trust sign announcing the Alnmouth Dunes property **E**. The path here is extremely well maintained and clearly signed. This area of the dunes is called Buston Links and from the rural

woodland bridge to the point where you turn inland by a long low building **F** is about a mile (1.5 km).

If you have time, do try to explore the intertidal area between this junction and the river estuary, from here it is possible to trace the original course of the Aln. You may even be able to work out how the large mound in front of you was once part of the town of Alnmouth, and how the former port here would have been well protected and quite spacious. The mound on which the town church stood is a good viewpoint.

The booklet *Exploring the Plantlife of the Northumberland Coast* (listed at the back of this guide) will be useful for identifying many of the plants along this coast.

Contours are given in metres
The vertical interval is 5 metres

There are signs here warning that it can be extremely dangerous to attempt crossing the river at any time, so, once you have explored this area, return to the junction described above F and go inland to join the cycleway, which is a very pleasant walkway as well, on a track separated from the road. This track turns towards Alnmouth and then towards the B1338 where it continues as a separate path to the bridge G over the River Aln. Once across the bridge, turn right along the river bank and keep going until you see the play area ahead of you. The official path turns left here and joins the street at which point you turn right, but it may be easier to step over the small sea defence wall and carry on through the recreation area.

Alnmouth was a port to which much of the grain from this area was sent for export by ship. Large granaries were built here, evidence of which can be found in the town at the Hindmarsh Hall in Northumberland Street, now the village hall. These granaries, along with an improved road system, were constructed as part of a plan devised by the Dukes of Northumberland to supply the grain from points inland.

The harbour scene is beautiful. There are quite a few boats scattered around the estuary and the plant life is particularly intriguing. In Alnmouth there is a range of accommodation and pubs. You might like to explore the town for a while, and there are information points telling you more about the history of the place. Before carrying on the coast make sure that it will not be high tide during the next

hour or so, since the path takes to a beach quite soon.

To continue northwards join or keep to the perimeter road, keeping the sandy beaches and then the golf course on your right and any buildings on your left. When you see a sign for the Beach Car Park H go down the separate footpath beside the road, have a look at the grand drinking fountain, and turn left along the footpath, the narrow path through the grass, which rises up into the dunes. If there has been heavy dew or it has been raining you may get rather soggy legs unless you are wearing waterproof gaiters.

At the top of the bank look back at wonderful views across Alnmouth Bay. There are some wartime defences here, which appear to have older foundations. Keep going north-east more or less on the level and you come to the edge of another golf course. Keep right of the fence and right of the ancient caravans in a field beside the path. When the track divides, the path going right is to the beach but take the left-hand one. You should now have Marden Rocks on your right and ahead of you a group of buildings, which is Foxton Hall, now the clubhouse for Alnmouth Golf Club I. The path is quite distinct here and shortly before you arrive at Foxton Hall you go left, just inland of the running fox wind vane.

Skirt round the inland side of the buildings. Then turn back towards the coast going left of the car park just beyond the gamekeeper's cottage and down the concrete track to the beach. There is a small morsel of cliff-top path

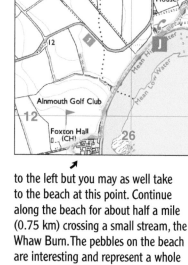

Contours are given in metres
The vertical interval is 5 metres

North Reins

Mar Mouth

Boulmer Haven

South Reins

Scotch Gap

Navigation Posts

Marmouth Scars

Airfield (disused)

Seaton Barns

Seaton Vale

Watch Hut

Broadroom End

Seaton House

Seaton Point

Bally Carrs

Brady Carrs

Alnmouth Golf Club

Foxton Hall (CH)

St Oswald's Way

N C Path

to the left but you may as well take to the beach at this point. Continue along the beach for about half a mile (0.75 km) crossing a small stream, the Whaw Burn. The pebbles on the beach are interesting and represent a whole range of geological formations in the county, some erratics from Scandinavia and probably stones of ballast from ships from other countries as well.

The cliff here is crumbling very fast but under the turf at the top of the cliff if you visit in late spring or early summer you may see a colony of sand martins feeding their young at their nests. Just after this there is a concrete flight of steps with iron railings J, which take you to the top of the cliff. The path continues along the top of the cliff just landward of a number of chalets. You

then come towards the buildings of Seaton House, built largely using the wind-blown desert sandstones found in this area. Bear right and go into the caravan site along a well-surfaced track. Where the track divides, bear left keeping the caravans on your right. Go through the kissing gate and continue along the short grassy track. Here there are duneland flowers including bloody cranesbill, a specialty of the Northumberland coast. If it is summer and the weather has been reasonable you will see some of the old cobles, the local fishing boats, moored in Boulmer Haven K.

The path continues through the dunes or along the track into Boulmer, which has a pub, the Coast Guard station and public toilets. As you leave Boulmer

you will enter the Howick Estate. For the next few miles the coast path will be very easy to follow, well signed, well surfaced and hardly in need of a description. The landscape gets wilder here and soon after you leave Boulmer you have the choice of keeping to the cliff edge around the headland or following the track. Amongst the rocks here you will see oystercatchers and herons, possibly being chased by the local crows. After 1.5 miles (2 km) the path crosses a footbridge and there is sign left to Howick Hillfort **L**, it is just across the field and worth a quick look. Keep on northwards following the cliff past the bathing house **N**. You pass a number of very attractive bays on this section and if you are interested in macro photography you will get some superb flower shots.

Howick Hall **M** is a 20-minute walk inland along the footpath and then the road, just north of Seahouses. It has beautiful gardens, an arboretum and tearooms. Well worth a visit. Leaflets are available in tourist

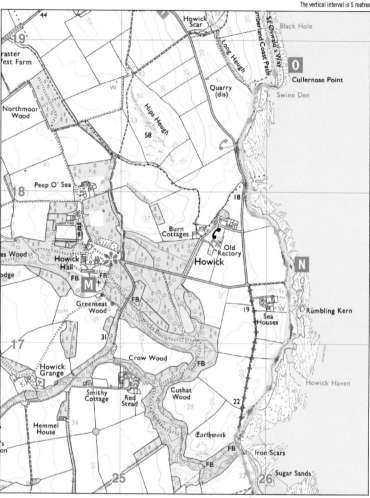

information centres and in lots of the local pubs, pick one up to check opening times, or go online at www.howickhallgardens.org

The next big feature going northwards is Cullernose Point O, a black whin sill outcrop with an impressive colony of kittiwakes on the cliff and spectacular flower displays on the cliff-top turf. Keep going for another mile close to the sea and you will be in Craster.

Craster has a pub P, a tourist information centre Q in a quarry just up the road, a smokery producing kippers which are distributed nationwide, a village shop and a rather good restaurant. The strange structures you see on the harbour are related to the quarrying, which took place here until recent times, with the stone being exported by boat. The bus stop is just up the road from the harbour.

Craster had three quarries, two limestone and one whinstone (now the car park). Some of the stone was crushed and taken down to the south pier on a pulley system. Big blocks of stone were taken to the north pier for shipping out. A range of other stone products were produced by the skilled quarrymen, including setts for street surfacing and curbstones. All the quarries had closed by the beginning of the Second World War. However, during the war stone was needed to build the runways at Boulmer and Burton Aerodromes and the quarries were re-opened in 1941. The first record of the quarrying is from 1772.

In 1947 there were two grocery shops, an off-licence, a butcher's, a hut that sold dressed crab, a market garden, two herring yards (L. Robson & Sons and Greys), and at least six cobles fishing from the harbour. Fishing was a big thing in Craster up until the 1970s, and the famous kippers have been smoked, packed into barrels and exported by sea for several generations. There are still several fishermen using the harbor, which is very charming.

If you do a search for Craster online there is a very interesting locally created website with the collected stories of peoples lives in the 20th century, as well as accounts of the known history of the village, and lots of old photos – definitely well worth a visit a visit.

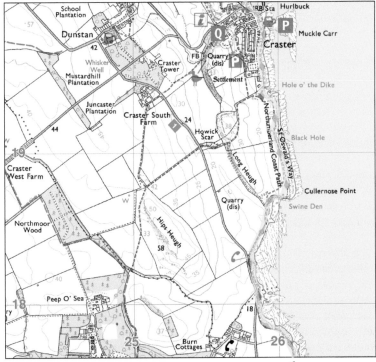

Contours are given in metres
The vertical interval is 5 metres

6 Craster to Seahouses

via Embleton and Beadnell

10 miles (16 km)

It's wild rocky shores with sandy beaches backed by dunes all the way, a number of good pubs, some camping sites and small 'havens' amongst the rocks with fishing hamlets nearby. There are photo opportunities at Embleton Bay with new angles on Dunstanburgh with a choice of rocky and sandy foregrounds. A detour to Embleton itself, with its mediaeval church and sturdy pele tower beside the churchyard is worthwhile. Some of the geological formations are works of art as well as of geological interest and the limekilns at Beadnell show that local coal shafts and supplies of limestone were put to good economic use, whilst the harbours built for this trade are still used for fishing and leisure. Don't forget to go into the old village at Craster and inspect the pub that was a pele tower and the intriguing church nearby.

To start the walk, go to the far side of the harbour and to the seaward side of the houses, and you're on the National Trust land all the way to Dunstanburgh Castle A. National Trust or English Heritage membership will get you in free, and there are information signs about the history. This magnificent landmark is well worth exploring inside. Like all the castles around here it sits on a dolerite, whinstone outcrop. Dunstanburgh Castle was built by Earl Thomas of Lancaster who fell out with the English King Edward II. The building of this castle was begun in 1313 on a massive scale, at a time when the Earl was actively plotting against the King. King Edward won the day and the Earl was executed nine years later. The story is much more complicated, but it hinges on the dissatisfaction of the nobles who had been supportive of Edward II's father and disapproved of his son's flippancy, inconsistency and weak rule. The castle was built largely to show the Earl's power.

John of Gaunt later took over the castle and fortified it against the Scots, including making the great twin-towered gatehouse into a keep. It did not feature particularly in battles against the Scots, but it was held by the Lancastrians (red rose) in the Wars of the Roses, during which much damage was done to the structure. It was never restored, became a ruin, and was robbed of its stone for building work in the surrounding area.

The artist William Turner. did some magnificent paintings of the castle in

the 1830s with pounding seas and dramatic skies, the castle caught by rays of sunlight in the background. One of them is called 'Wreckers, Coast of Northumberland' and is currently in the Yale Centre for British Art in the USA. Apparently Turner went out to paint at dawn, when the light would have been coming from the east. Photographers please note: it now features in every coffee-table book of photos of the Northumberland coast as well as frequently in photographic magazines. Some of the best shots are from the

northern side towards sunset.

The coast path goes inland of the castle enclosure, through a valley behind. You get some interesting views of the castle and the rocks it stands on and you come out on the stony beach with an unusual geological formation, which looks like a wave, called, Greymare Rock B. About 12 minutes walk past this you come to a road at Dunston Steads with some parking spaces. Continue behind the dunes to the golf clubhouse C directly below Embleton

Turner's viewpoint for
his Dunstanburgh Castle
sketches and paintings.

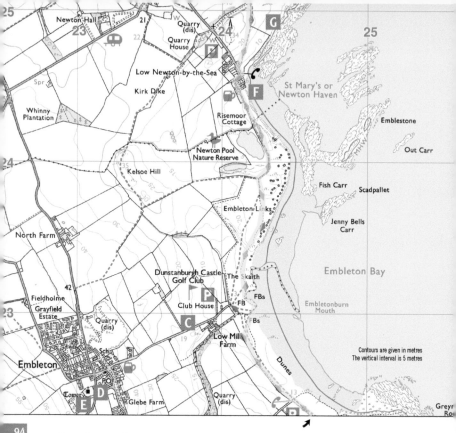

where there is also parking. Walkers are welcome to share the facilities for eating and drinking in the clubhouse and you can pay for parking.

If you go up the road here to Embleton go straight over the first junction and walk a few yards along the B1339 to the village church **D**. The interior is worth an inspection. On your left, as you enter the church, is an ancient pele tower **E**. It is adjacent to the former vicarage and such pele towers were called vicar's or parson's peles. (The word pele or peel comes from the word for an enclosure, originally a word for a stake.) We know that this tower was built in 1385 for £40 following a Scottish raid. The crenellations were added in the 15th century to give the structure a bit of class.

You will see pele towers at Beadnell, where the Craster Arms includes one, on the Farne Islands and you will have already seen one at Cresswell. There are scores of these structures, mainly in Northumberland and Cumberland. They were built from the late 13th century until the beginning of the 17th century. During this 300-year period the border reivers (the word comes from robber and still exists in the word ruffian), both Scots and English gangs used to set out on lawless raids, ransacking villages, stealing whole herds of sheep and cattle, and generally making a living from stealing other people's possessions. These towers, normally with a vaulted ground floor and very thick walls, had a room above accessible only through the vaults and

The heavily fortified pele tower by Embleton Church.

were built throughout the area. If you want to see inside one, Preston Tower is open to the public, 7 miles (11 km) north of Alnwick, signed off the A1. Alternatively visit the Craster Arms in Beadnell.

The kings of England and Scotland made various attempts through the centuries to regulate the activities of the border reivers, usually without success. Eventually, after the union of England and Scotland, King James made strenuous efforts to wipe out their power. They were imprisoned, hanged, deported to Ireland or, finally, scripted into the army and sent to fight in foreign lands. By about 1680 things began to settle down and the construction of such buildings was no longer necessary.

Having visited Embleton, return to Embleton Bay and continue north to Low Newton-by-the-Sea (National Trust). Here there is another haven, often with boats moored in it, and the Ship Inn **F** where the excellent food can be eaten outdoors. Note there is a public telephone box here. From experience, few of the mobile phone operators reached this point with their signals. There is a car park a little further up the road where visitors are required to park their cars. The village square is car free except for those renting accommodation here.

From the square go back up the road and turn right along the grassy path across Newton Point **G**. This is also National Trust land. Continue along behind the dunes on the

a risk of disturbing the terns. So cross the bridge and continue along the path around the bay to Beadnell Harbour H. As you come towards Beadnell Harbour you will be walking through a caravan site and will come to a car park. From here you can either walk along the road a little farther and turn right to Beadnell Harbour, or you can walk across the beach.

well-maintained path until you come to the bridge over the Brunton Burn. Outside of the tern nesting season you can cross the beach here, but as you will probably be walking here during the spring or summer you are asked not to go onto the dunes where there is

Beadnell is not to be underestimated by first impressions. The harbour is very attractive and has ancient limekilns owned by the National Trust, cobles moored in the harbour, a beautiful 18th-century church, and a pub, the Craster Arms I, which incorporates a pele tower.

Coble moored by the lime kilns at Beadnall Harbour.

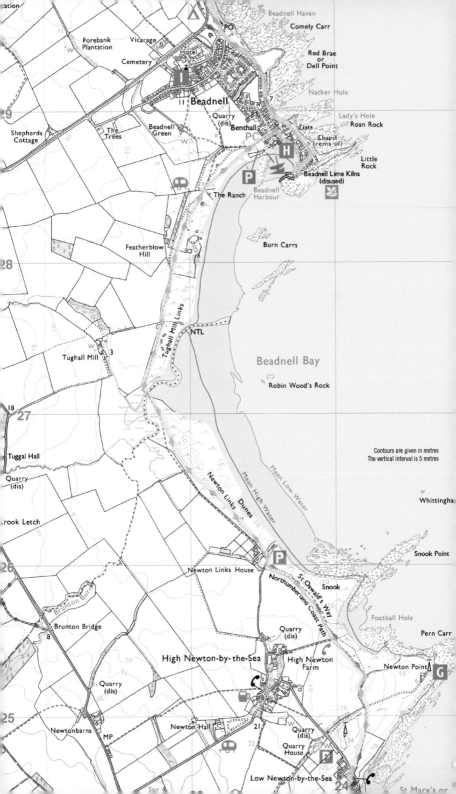

Contours are given in metres
The vertical interval is 5 metres

The limekilns on the coast in this part of Northumberland were built following the agricultural revolution in the 18th century. The importance of applying lime to the fields in order to improve the crops was the main reason for the explosion in lime production during the 18th and 19th centuries. Lime had of course been used at least since Roman times as a mortar, but the Agricultural Revolution meant that far larger quantities were demanded in order to increase food production for a rapidly growing population in the British Isles.

Much of the stone on the beach and just inland between Beadnell and Seahouses, as well as at Craster, is limestone. There are also seams of coal in the area, which initially was sufficient to fire these kilns. It was difficult to work, and not vast in quantity, but coal would have been brought in from coal mines further south as that became a problem.

The limekilns that you see at Beadnell are the first of a series of industrial-scale structures which were built primarily in the early years of the 19th century, ceasing production at the end of the century. The reason for this was that establishment of a railway system meant that limekilns could be operated anywhere on a railway. Before that time, the only transport of such heavy goods would have been by boat, hence structures of this date are only found near or at coastal ports. You will be seeing similar structures at Seahouses and Lindisfarne. You may recognise other, smaller-scale, limekilns along the coast.

To get to Seahouses from Beadnell walk along the low cliff top, either on the road or on the paths, until you get to the junction of the B1340. Here you can find your way down to the beach and walk along it to Seahouses. There is a stream to cross at the far end, but most walkers have no problem with this as long as the tide is not too high. Check the tide tables online, in the booklets that are likely to be on sale or check on your phone app.

Otherwise walk along the roadside on the recently provided pavement along the back of the dunes. There is a Camping and Caravanning Club site at the beginning of the walk, which could be useful if you're camping.

If you are on the beach, cross the stream at the northern end of the beach I and look for a path over the rocks and into the golf course. Follow the signs through the golf course, which makes excellent provision for walkers, and keep as close to the sea as you can all the way to Seahouses Harbour J.

Seahouses has a reputation for chip shops and too many visitors. Visitors, however, are vital to the economy of this part of Northumberland. There are lots of shops, a post office, some good pubs (look them up in a reliable pub guide before you get there), a port full of fishing boats, an interesting smokery that is still operating and open to customers and visitors, a lifeboat station and the RNLI sculpture. The little structure out on the rocks is the gunpowder store used when the harbour was being built.

Fishing in Seahouses is still a lively scene, but with North Sea fish stocks declining it is nothing like it used to be. However, the fishermen can diversify to some extent by installing safety

At Seahouses the proximity of coal mines, limestone and sea transport led to these industrial-scale limekilns being built in the 19th century. Now they are used for storage, and the boats take visitors to the Farne Islands.

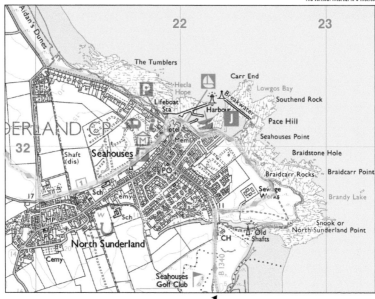

equipment and seats on the boats or investing in purpose-built craft, and taking visitors out to the Farne Islands for a variety of activities. Some like to go and watch the birds on Staple Island and/or Inner Farne. This you can do for a morning or an afternoon and, depending on your degree of interest, a grand all-day trip. Photographers with a telephoto lens will find plenty to do on a two-island trip lasting all day.

The National Trust manages the two islands with great skill in order to protect nesting sites of the terns, puffins, guillemots, razorbills, shags and kittiwakes, and you can get superb photos of any of the species if you venture out.

If you're not so interested, but would like to have a look, you can visit one island or perhaps take a cruise without landing to see the birds flying overhead and watch the seals basking on the rocks. In the next chapter I shall give you some details of the variety of trips that you can take. Of course there are also fishing trips for keen fishermen.

The limekilns here are quite spectacular and are used by the RNLI and fishermen for storage, as they often are elsewhere along the coast. Here too, the coal was mined nearby and taken from the cliffs (where you can see it still) and later supplies from elsewhere were brought in by boat and then by rail. There was enough limestone available from the immediate surroundings for the whole lifetime of the operation.

In the next chapter I'm going to describe the vital coastal walks and boat trips available on and around the Farne Islands, which are of course parts of the Northumberland coast.

Fishing boats at Seahouses now used to ferry visitors to the Farne Islands.

7 The Farne Islands

Including Staple, Inner Farne and Longstone.

The Farne Islands National Nature Reserve is managed by the National Trust. There are, roughly speaking, between 15 and 28, islands according to the state of the tide, of which you can normally visit three: Staple, Inner Farne and Longstone. The main breeding colonies are there in May, June and July. Soon after the end of July they migrate south for the winter, returning the following spring and are only rarely seen here.

The islands are about 3 miles (5 km) away from the mainland and 6 miles (10 km) south of Holy Island. All the sea trips run from Seahouses Harbour and there is a group of kiosks on the quayside where you can buy your tickets. The tourist information centre will also give you information on the variety of trips available, or you can use the websites and phone numbers at the end of this guide under Useful Information. Some of the boats, which are owned by a variety of firms, concentrate on particular islands and

Longstone Lighthouse.

Knivestone

Northern
Hares
Humber
Rock   Longstone
                                        The Hopper
Sunderland Hole
                Clove Car
                Little Harcar   Blue Caps
North
Wamses   Big Harcar

South Wamses   Roddam and Green

                Brownsman Haven

Oscar or   Brownsman
South Goldstone

Farne Islands
(NORTHUMBERLAND
NORTH SUNDERLAND CP)   Pinnacles Haven

                Gun Rock   Staple Island

Megstone   Farne Islands
                National Nature Reserve   Skeney Scar

                                            Callers
                                                Crumstone
37 ────────── Staple Sound

                Knocklin Ends

            Knoxes Reef
Solan Rock   Longcar Hole
St Cuthberts Gut
                Newbiggin Bush
The Kettle
Churn Gut   Farne
            Haven   Scarcar   Little Scarcar
36   The Churn   Oxscar   Big Scarcar   The Bush
            West   East
            Widopens   Widopens
    Inner Farne   The Thorn

Inner Sound

35

Greenhill
Rocks
34

Monks House
Rocks

Shoreston
Rocks

33
Shoreston
Hall
        Shaft
        (dis)

North   The Tumblers   Cart End
Cottage   Lowgate Bay
                    Lifeboat   Southend Rock
                    Sta
NORTH SUNDERLAND CP   Harbour   Pace Hill
Shaft   Seahouses Point
(dis)   Seahouses
Westfield   Braidstone Hole

                            Braidcarr Rocks   Braidcarr Point
                        Sewage
                        Works   Brandy Lake

                                    Snook or
            CH   North Sunderland Point
North Sunderland   Old
                    Shells
Corry

        Seahouses
        Golf Club
                NTL
        Annstead
        Bridge   Annstead
31   Rocks

Southfield
                Annstead
                Farm   23
        Lodge   Annstead

Contours are given in metres
The vertical interval is 5 metres

24   25

activities. Be careful to choose exactly what you want. I shall give a few examples to give you an idea of the range of trips, which might be available on the day of your visit.

Longstone Island

Some of the trips go to Longstone Island **A**, the former home of Grace Darling and her family. Some just circle the island. Some land on the island and you have a chance to walk around and see the lighthouse from outside as well as possibly getting quite close, but not too close, to the seals. Good for photo opportunities, if you are lucky.

Golden Gate run trips, which include landing on the island and visits to the lighthouse interior.

Grace Darling was born in 1815 in Bamburgh. Her father, William, was the keeper at the former lighthouse on Brownsman Island **B**. As you are sailing past Brownsman you'll see a house, now used as a base for the National Trust rangers, and if you look carefully behind it you'll see the base of a former lighthouse. Brownsman is actually joined on to Staple Island **C** at low tide. Brownsman also has some soil on the island and William Darling was able to keep an allotment there to provide fresh vegetables. Later the decision was made to construct a lighthouse on Longstone Island for a more effective warning system, and the family had to move. Longstone has no soil, so nowhere to grow any vegetables. Some feel that

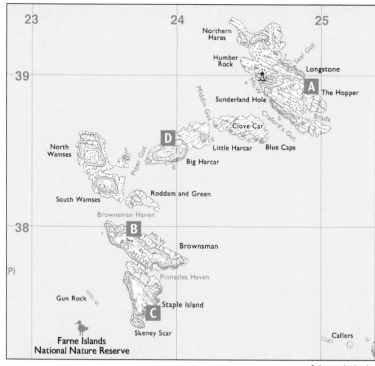

Contours are given in metres
The vertical interval is 5 metres

Grace Darling's poor health and early death could well have been related to malnutrition as well as the difficult conditions on the island.

Looking out to sea, Longstone Lighthouse is the one painted red and white. Grace Darling's bedroom window looked out from the white section in the middle. On 7 September 1838 she saw from this room a shipwreck and survivors on the low rocky island known as Big Harcar **D** across extremely rough seas. Grace and her father decided that the weather would prevent their lifeboat putting out from Seahouses (then called North Sunderland), so rowed out and first rescued four men and one woman who were still alive. With the help of these survivors her father then rowed back to the island and brought more passengers to safety in the Longstone Lighthouse. The lifeboat did eventually get out, but by the time it arrived there were no more survivors. The sea was so rough that the lifeboat made for the lighthouse, where the Darlings and the survivors had to remain for three days before the sea calmed down enough to enable them to return. There is a museum in Bamburgh, which you must visit to find out the rest of the

Puffins have a special joint which enables them to hold multiple fish for their young.

Young seal shedding its fur coat in preparation for life in the ocean.

story. Grace Darling is buried in the churchyard at Bamburgh and there is a memorial to her inside the church.

Do make sure that if you want to visit the lighthouse you choose the right boat, or if you merely want to walk around the island, a really remote and beautiful spot, take a boat that lands only. There may be a waiting seal pup on the steps when you arrive. You are warned to keep your distance, but they are curious and may well pose for a quick photo if you have a medium telephoto lens.

The National Trust claims that the Farne Islands are the most exciting seabird colony in England. I think they could be right. There are 23 species of bird to be seen including massive numbers of puffins. There is also the grey seal colony with more than 1,000 pups born every autumn. You will also see some common seals (or harbour seals) amongst them. If you are doing the walk in the autumn then there will be no large breeding colonies on the islands, but there will be seals. A visit to Longstone and/ or a non-landing circuit of the islands could be worthwhile. Bear in mind when planning your trip that there are

An Arctic tern prepares to attack my camera on Inner Farne.

Inner Farne

When you land on Inner Farne **E** in spring, you will be greeted by the Arctic terns. Wear a strong hat, or two, and be ready to put it in the washing machine as soon as you return to base. They will ardently defend their nesting sites and are quite ready to give you a peck if your head is uncovered. They have dark red bills and are great acrobats. If you have a fast camera you may get some good shots of individuals taken against the sky, catching the light through their white wings. Group shots with the chapel in the background can also be good. They migrate from Southern Africa to the Northumberland coast annually; the most immense journey. Most visitors enjoy encountering them and can see the funny side of things. Try not to get agitated and angry, it can spoil the visit. Also be very careful not to tread on the birds' eggs whilst you're distracted by their parents.

As you come up from the pier there are the remains of some buildings on your left, which are all that remains of St Cuthbert's hospitium, where his visitors used to stay.

As you come away from the ferry you can turn left towards the lighthouse, to start inspecting the breeding grounds or you can go straight ahead into the little courtyard inside the chapel. On your left is a small information centre where the rangers are usually available to answer questions and generally help you. They post details of all bird sightings on the island and there is lots of other information available in the hut. To the right is the chapel dedicated

days when stormy weather can mean no trips run. You may have to make arrangements to return here on another day, so build that into your plans.

Staple Island

Staple Island **C** should be visited primarily if you want to see the puffins, razorbills, guillemots, kittiwakes, cormorants and shags. The single visit, one-hour trips will enable you to see all the birds – and pretty exciting it is too. If you really want to get some good photographs, relax a bit, and feel you want to explore, then the two-hour trip is a better bet. There will be National Trust rangers there, who can answer your questions about the birds. There is a new landing on the seaward side of the island, which doubles your chances of being able to land in slightly choppy conditions. The National Trust rangers will have staked out the area which you can visit and visiting times are limited to prevent disturbance to the birds as this can hinder successful breeding. Staple Island is joined on to Brownsman where you'll see the house and old lighthouse where the Darling family lived before going to Longstone.

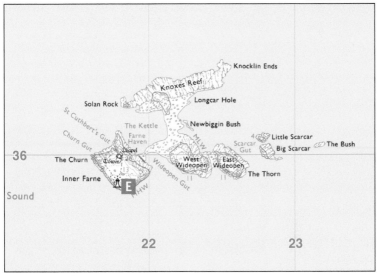

to St Cuthbert, who lived on the island from 678 to 684. I shall be giving you more details of his life when we get to Lindisfarne. This chapel was built in the 13th century when it was a small Benedictine community of two monks and a few servants. These monks grew their own vegetables on the island, bred poultry and livestock, sold fish, sea bird eggs, fish and seal oil as well as recycling anything landing on the island including items from wrecked ships. Henry III donated a piece of land roughly halfway between Seahouses and Bamburgh, and here was built Monks House, which was used as a store supplies to and from the island. This still appears on the maps, and you will see it by the stream if you follow the beach to get from Seahouses to Bamburgh.

By the middle of the 19th century the chapel had lost its roof and the archdeacon of Durham Cathedral, Charles Thorp, became concerned about the building. Seventeenth-century woodwork from Durham Cathedral was then installed in the church and is still there today. The stained-glass windows and alter furnishings were fitted by well-known craftsmen of the 19th century. The main fabric of the chapel is mediaeval and contemporary with the monks' occupation.

Coming out of the chapel, on your right, is another pele tower. Prior Thomas Castell of Durham had it built in 1500 supposedly on the site of St Cuthbert's cell. Presumably the occupants of the island were in need of protection from the reivers at that time. During the time of Elizabeth I it was used as a fort. In the late 17th century Charles II granted a licence for the first lighthouse to be established here, but the merchants of Newcastle refused to support it financially and no light was ever lit on this building. Now the National Trust uses the building as rangers' accommodation and it is not open to the public.

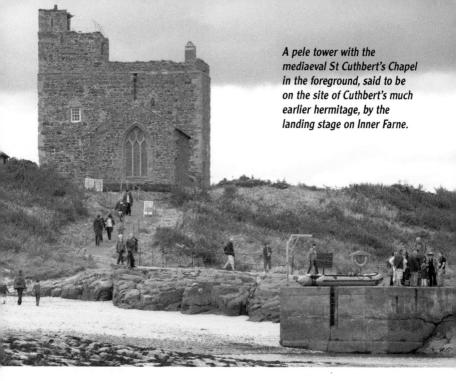

A pele tower with the mediaeval St Cuthbert's Chapel in the foreground, said to be on the site of Cuthbert's much earlier hermitage, by the landing stage on Inner Farne.

The present lighthouse on Inner Farne, with accommodation for keepers, was built in 1811. It is powered by solar units and remotely controlled from Harwich.

Our main reason for coming here, in addition to the historical interest of Anglo-Saxon and mediaeval occupation, is the spectacular colony of nesting birds.

Go up the path towards the lighthouse, which you leave to your right. As you pass it the attacks from the Arctic terns diminish and you start to see the altogether more polite puffins standing around their nests, flying in with the fish, and darting down their burrows to make sure all is well with their chicks. Early in the season you may not see them bringing in fish, but they will still be hanging around in the nest and caring for the eggs below. If you are

taking photographs try and get one of them flying around and landing, that's much more fun than photos of them just standing there. You will not need the ultimate in telephoto lenses. They are so close that a normal telephoto zoom will easily capture them.

As you reach the cliffs, the numbers of puffins increase. You will also see shags, cormorants, kittiwakes, guillemots and razorbills. A percentage of the guillemots here have an attractive white stripe on their bills, and are referred to as bridled. But most guillemots have fairly straightforward bills and slightly greyer feathers than the razorbills (who definitely have attitude).

The guillemots like to be in colonies, as do the puffins, and the razorbills tend to be alone or in smaller groups. All three species of these birds, referred to as auks (after their family), disappear at the beginning of August and travel quite long distances to good fishing grounds, only to return to dry land at the beginning of the next breeding season. Research is currently being done using GPS into where exactly they do go. Certainly you will rarely see any auks close to land outside the nesting season. Occasionally in winter little auks are seen, especially when conditions in the Arctic become extremely cold.

There are shags and cormorants here. The cormorants generally have a white patch on the chin, whilst the shags are smaller, have a yellow patch, often have a crest, and a green sheen when the sun shines on them. Otherwise their habits are similar. The shags outnumber the cormorants on these islands substantially.

There are three species of tern breeding here. The aggressive Arctic tern with its all-red bill is described above. The common tern has a red bill with a black tip. The sandwich tern has a yellow bill with a black tip, and a shaggy crest. The common and sandwich terns migrate annually to the North African coast for winter sun.

The kittiwakes have yellow bills and you will see them clinging onto the cliffs with their chicks around them on the nest in seemingly impossible positions. If you started the walk in Newcastle in the spring or summer you will have seen them clinging on to the Tyne Bridge and other structures in the centre of the city. You will also have seen them at Cullernose Point just

These basalt stacks on Inner Farne are amongst the most popular nesting sites.

north of Howick. Unlike many of the other birds the kittiwakes do not move very far outside the breeding season and some may be seen all year round. They feed on sand eels, which come to the surface of the North Sea during late evening and remain there until early morning. Presumably the ones that have settled in the centre of Newcastle go to the North Sea to carry out their fishing each day.

During your boat trip you'll also see the gannets passing and, as you go further north, you'll see these large white birds flying in groups or singly with great purpose, occasionally rising to great heights and diving at high

Razorbill

Eider Duck

speed. I'll tell you more about these when we reach Lindisfarne, as they actually breed on Bass Rock, over the Scottish border, there are more on the island north of the Farne Islands.

If you are keeping an eye out for roseate terns (black bills, endangered species) a few individuals may be seen but none breed here. The place to see them is Coquet Island – boat trips from Amble leave daily in season, subject to weather. Ring Amble TIC for details (further Information at the back of this book).

Below are the round figures for the main breeding birds you will see on the Farne Islands during May, June and July, based on 2011/12 counts:

- Puffin – 72,000
- Guillemot – 50,000
- Black-legged kittiwake (yellow bill, nests on precipices) – 8,000
- Arctic tern (dark red bill, aggressive) – 2,000
- Sandwich tern (yellow bill with black tip, shaggy crest) – 2,000
- Shag (yellow chin, green sheen, crest often visible) – 2,000
- Eider (see photo) – 1,000
- Black-headed gull (curved wings in flight, black heads in summer, black dot behind eye in winter) – 900
- Razorbill (see photo) – 800
- Fulmar (very unusual bills with large nostrils, flat-winged flight and much gliding) – 500
- Cormorant (black with white patch on chin) – 270
- Common tern (red bill with black tip) – 180

Photographers could aim to get all these species on the all-day tours if their travelling companions will allow it. You can get so close on these islands that a 70-200 mm lens should be sufficient for all the shots. If you take a super telephoto your shoulders will ache by the end of the day, and you'll get mainly head and shoulder shots only. Remember to get some action in the shots for dynamic, sometimes comic, effect or if you want to win any competitions. Grey days can be just as good as sunny days, and the reduced contrast can help stop the bright white feathers bleaching out.

The grey seals feed on fish taken at depths down to 230 feet (70 metres). (Gannets can only dive to 65 feet (20 metres).) If necessary grey seals will also take crustaceans. The average daily food requirement is estimated to be 11 lb (5 kg), although seals do not feed every day and fast during the breeding season.

Grey seals are the largest breeding seals found in the UK. Over half of the world's population of grey seals are found around British coasts, and numbers here have doubled since 1960. The breeding sites are called rookeries. Pups weigh 14 kg at birth, but since their mother's milk contains 60 per cent fat, they quickly develop the blubber layer essential for maintaining

Seal pup on Longstone Island.

body temperature out at sea. Pups are born with white 'puppy' fur, which they moult after about three weeks, the white coat is not waterproof so the pups first swim after it has been shed.

Male grey seals reach maturity at six years and females at three to five years. The latter give birth to their pups in the autumn and early winter. The first British pups are born off the Isles of Scilly and Cornwall in August and September, and the time of pupping is progressively later as you move clockwise around the British Isles, the latest pups being born off the east coast of Scotland and then here on the Farne Islands in late December.

Seals can swim many miles when foraging, they have even been known to make trips to the Netherlands and back within a few days

Blubber gives their bodies a streamlined surface for fast underwater action and it is an excellent insulating layer, superior to hair in the water. It does not get thinner under pressure and retains its insulating properties at depth, allowing seals to live in waters only slightly above freezing. In young pups, hair is still the primary insulator until a layer of blubber is produced.

In the wild, males may live for about 25 years, females for about 35, with man being the major predator. In Britain, hunting for seals for food has been carried out for millenia, and by 1914 only 500 grey seals were thought to be left. Laws passed in 1914 and 1970 limited hunting to outside the breeding season, allowing grey seal numbers to recover, leading to conflict with some fishermen. The grey seal was in fact the first British mammal to be given legal protection. Seal culls were carried out in the 1960s and 1970s, but have since then ceased due to lack of proof that seal numbers affect catches. Seals are still shot legally all year round if caught near fishing nets.

8 Seahouses to Belford

via Bamburgh and Budle
11.7 miles (18.6 km)

The official route from Seahouses to Belford goes inland after Seahouses, again at Budle Bay, and becomes quite challenging. If you enjoy wallowing around in slippery mud, making your way through crops, crossing a high-speed railway line on trestles and risking the A1 then you will find the official route exciting and rewarding. On this inland section there are a few good views from the hills and one or two possibly iron age earthworks. If it has been raining more than usual you'll need waterproof footwear for mud (there is one particularly muddy descent at Spindlestone Heughs) and the path is likely to be flooded and overgrown in places. At the time of writing waymarks are intermittent, some of the stiles and gates are rotten or broken, and signs can be faded. You will need the description and maps in this guide to find your way. On the Seahouses to Belford walk you may get away with dodging the flooded sections and, with luck, guessing how deep the mud or flood is, but I will suggest an alternative on tracks and roads where you may find duck ponds have taken over the line of the right of way. On the Belford to Fenwick section (Chapter 9) there will not be any ponds to cross, but it may be muddy, and some of the streams have no bridges. Waterproof socks, wellies or combat boots and walking poles might make life less uncomfortable. If this does not grab you, find 'Bamburgh to Budle on the beaches and cliff tops route' on page 121.

Seahouses to Belford – the official route (inland)

From Seahouses Harbour go inland from the boat trip kiosks up to the dramatic 'Rescue' sculpture of a lifeboat crew member A. Cross the road and go towards the centre. When you see the tourist information office opposite B, turn right and make your way down through the car park. When you see the rubbish bins make for a gate in the right-hand corner and go through it.

After rain this section of the path can be flooded but you should be able to skip along the edge here and there and get through without getting too wet. This is the old Seahouses railway line, which you follow until you reach the next road C.

The official path then goes right, along the verge, for a few yards. Then on the opposite side of the road you will see a stone stile leading into a field. (Local people taking a walk and runners I passed were using the lane opposite rather than the footpath because they said it was not easy to get through. If you do this, following the national cycleway, take the first turning right and you will come to the group of buildings which you are making for.)

The official footpath goes diagonally across the field and to the left of a barbed-wire fence, which is in a corner of the adjacent field. Then head for a stile that takes you into two normally arable fields and towards a group of buildings mentioned above, which are to the south-west of Shoreston Hall D. You are making, roughly speaking, for the middle of that group of buildings, and will find a stone stile leading you into the lane

there. At the time of writing the field had crops across the path and full waterproof clothing was needed to enable a dry crossing.

Once in the lane there is some easy walking ahead. Turn right for a few yards and then left and follow the lane north-west past Saddlershall E, keeping to the tarmac road until you reach Fowberry F. Here there is a farmyard and a small caravan site. Turn right along a track until it comes out in a field. Turn left along the field edge, then go left through a galvanised gate, and cross the stream – Ingram Burn. Now follow the wall and keep more or less straight ahead until you see the group of buildings and a white gabled house with a chimney on your

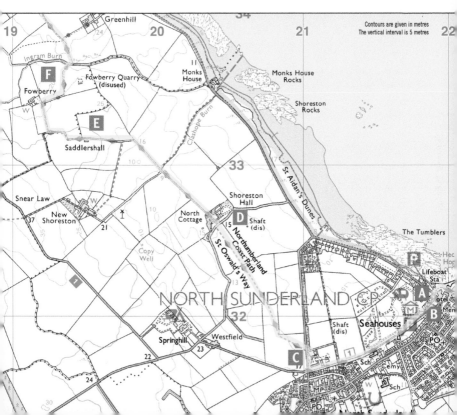

right. This is called Red Barn House G. Go to the right of the house through the overgrown corner of the field. Then go to the right of the wall and down the narrow path alongside the house, which can be overgrown with nettles. Look for a bridle gate opposite and go straight ahead through the end of a garden, then continue straight on and cross the drive to go through a kissing gate into a large field. You are aiming for the woods to the left of the red-tiled houses. When you get closer to the woods you will see a small building with a chimney H, which could have been a smithy.

Go to the left of the cattle trough in the middle of the field and keep going towards the building with a chimney.

When you arrive, there are several gates and these will take you on to the main road.

Turn left into Bamburgh. There is a good pavement on the road. The first thing you will come to is Bamburgh Castle on the right. This might be a good time for a visit, which is well worthwhile. Bamburgh has all the facilities you will need for a night's stay if you have booked ahead. The views of the castle from around the village are marvellous, especially in the evening when the castle is floodlit. If you make a point of going round the interior of the castle it will be all the more rewarding because you know what you're looking at.

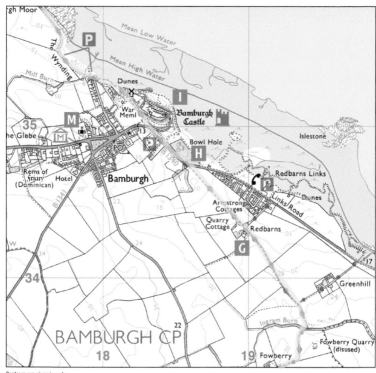

Contours are given in metres
The vertical interval is 5 metres

Bamburgh Castle from the north, in the evening.

Bamburgh Castle

The Norman castle with its keep I, probably built by Henry II, is imposing on top of its whin sill, basalt, outcrop. This outcrop has been used as a defensive lookout for millennia, and research is currently going on to find out what lies beneath the Norman castle. Visiting the castle will give you more information about this research. What we do know is that the Anglo-Saxon state of Bernicia, a kingdom running from the Humber to the Forth, was ruled from this castle. This is the kingdom that gave Northumberland (land north of the Humber) its name. One of the kings, named Oswald, was keen to convert the population to Christianity and engaged the help of the monks at the Holy Isle of Iona, then occupied by Celtic Christians.

As other powers nibbled away at the southern part of this kingdom, and as the Scots moved the northern border south, eventually settling on the Tweed at Berwick-upon-Tweed, Northumberland, the kingdom north of

The magnificent Bamburgh Castle at night.

the humber, became the area between the Tyne and the Tweed. With more recent local government reorganisations, the independent councils of North Tyneside and Newcastle occupy the more heavily populated areas, leaving Northumberland as one of the most sparsely populated counties in England.

The Normans built and maintained this castle in order to keep pressure on the Scottish kings and nobles. Eventually, during the Wars of the Roses, the castle walls were destroyed and it was never used as a defensive outpost again.

At one stage Lord Crewe, Bishop of Durham, made some efforts to conserve the castle, but the grand building that we now see is largely a creation of the famous engineer, William Armstrong (1st Lord Armstrong), who engaged architects to create a house where he could resort from time to time, with a fine great hall and wonderful views. The castle is still in the possession of the Armstrong family who welcome the public, keep it floodlit in summer and are successfully maintaining the structure. There is a café in the castle, a variety of historical exhibits, and the King's Hall is available for weddings. The mediaeval

church J is worth a visit as is the Grace Darling Museum M, and if you are feeling hungry or thirsty there are pubs, teashops, and other outlets in the village. I would recommend spending at least a morning or an afternoon, possibly an overnight stay, exploring Bamburgh.

Continuing along the Coast Path ...

The official path and my recommendations for the trek from Bamburgh to Budle are similar. The only place where the official path can be impossible to negotiate is immediately under Bamburgh Castle. It is well signed, but sometimes totally overgrown. The easiest solution is to go onto the beach and walk along it left and north until you see a country lane on the top of the cliff. Follow the lane past the lighthouse until you come to the Bamburgh Castle Golf Course K. If the tide is high, the alternative is to go up the road away from the castle and take the first right. This is the country lane that leads to the golf course.

At the entrance to the golf club, by the clubhouse, is a wooden sign saying 'Public Bridleway', 'Budle Point ¾' and

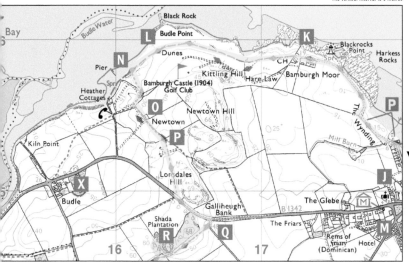

'Coast Path'. (You may choose to follow another sign down to the beach where there is the odd bit of scrambling across rocks to go west to Budle Point L. As long as you go at low tide there should be no problems and most of the walk will be sandy beaches. To rejoin the inland official route go back up the dunes by the pier N, which you come to after Budle point, go south-east and briefly into the caravan site turning left towards the cottages at Newtown.)

If you are staying on the cliff top follow the signs and blue posts, which the golf club has installed, and you should have no problems. The path stays fairly near the cliff top, sometimes on the grassy path and sometimes following a stone track. There is quite a lot of yellow lady's bedstraw, once used in coaching inns to make the foul straw in the sleeping areas smell better, and also heather beside this path.

When you see the pier on your right, go inland and then into the caravan

site. As you go down through the caravan site you will see a gate on your left and the track going towards some houses O. The right of way on the map is shown going between the houses, but this is now obstructed and the track takes you around the right-hand side of the buildings. Go around to the back of the buildings and continue on the line of the original track and you come back onto the golf course.

As you re-enter the golf course through a wooden kissing gate P one path goes diagonally left and the other diagonally right. Take the branch leading right and follow the blue posts up the hill crossing the short length of surfaced track, you will see a set of steps with handrails on the right which formed a lookout for the golfers. Go to the left of this and you will find a grassy path going straight on next to one of the blue posts. Keep straight on in the direction that you have been going since you left the gate giving access to this part of the golf course. You'll

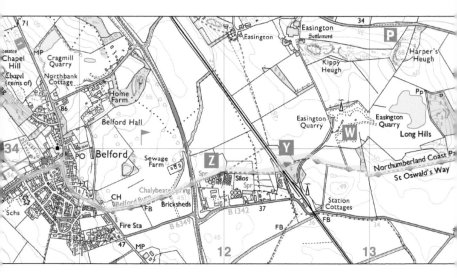

come to one final golf green and see a brown wooden field gate with a bridal gate on its right.

When you go through this you will be on the Bamburgh to Budle Road (and bus route). Turn left down the wide grassy verge. You will see another outcrop of basalt, which has been cut away to provide you with this grassy verge to walk along.

Take the next turning right and immediately turn right again through a wooden kissing gate Q. There is a wooden sign saying 'Public Footpath', 'Spindlestone Heughs' and 'Coast Path'. 'Heughs' means quarries in this case and is pronounced (I am told) 'hew'.

Aim to the left of a small wood R, which lies straight ahead, and keep going straight on over a new stile by the woods. Continue more or less straight on over another stile, which consists of two steps with a handle to hold on to. This crosses some barbed wire encased in a water pipe. Keep

straight on along the edge of the field until you come to a road. Turn left along the road for a very short distance and then right. At the end of this road there is a sharp bend left. There is a caravan site here, Waren Mill Caravan Park S, with a bar and refreshments available next to the entrance. The public footpath is shown as crossing the caravan site to the far left-hand corner of this field. If you negotiate your way through the caravans to the far left bottom corner of the field you will find a bridle gate with two waymark arrows pointing right.

You are now going to go down the valley through a grassy field with some woods behind a stone wall on your right. You then go through a metal gate and into coppice woodland. Still beside the wall keep straight on along the right-hand edge of a large field. Water can collect at the bottom of the field, where the path is, and you may have to walk around the standing water. The path beyond that point can also be flooded, but a way round can still

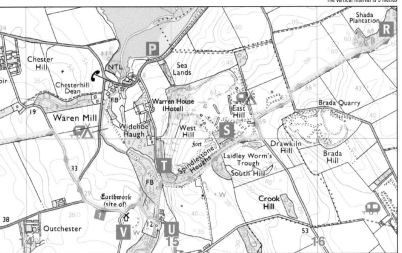

be negotiated. The path then branches off right into the woods. The descent through the woods is, after rain, a steep mud bath with no provision for walkers. If you have walking poles with you they may be helpful. It will still be difficult, and you may get very muddy indeed. At the bottom of this ordeal you come to a country lane T.

Turn left along the lane past some houses to Spindlestone Mill U, which is now flats. Turn right here across the river, the Waren Burn, and go up the hill until you see a former windmill V, now holiday accommodation. You may be able to make out the ancient, possibly prehistoric, earthwork around this building.

Turn right, following the Coast and Castles cycleway National Route 1 and keep straight on at the next two junctions as you briefly follow the B1342 (the Coast and Castles bus route). Halfway down a long stretch of straight lane you will see, if you look carefully, a sign in the hedge pointing

across the fields to the left. Keeping the hedge field boundary on your left, tramp through the overgrown headland of this arable field, under high voltage electricity cables. At one point there is a wall crossing on a very rotten ladder stile. There is a brief right and left, but keep going in the same direction along a traceable path, and you come to a quarry track that used to serve the now derelict Easington Quarry W. Continue straight ahead at the next sharp bend, still following the overhead cables.

The only other walker I met who had risen to the challenge of walking this part of the path turned down the quarry track left at the next corner and continued towards Belford over the road railway crossing, and into Belford on the pavement beside that road. After reading the description of the next section, you may decide to do likewise.

The official path carries straight on at the bend, crosses a closed railway line that served the quarry, and then crosses the King's Cross to Edinburgh main line Y.

Almost all of the passenger trains at this point are doing 125 mph (200 kph), that's a mile every 30 seconds, in both directions. So make sure you cross the line in less than 30 seconds, and don't trip on the roughly laid trestles that are there to help you over the crossing point.

Be absolutely sure to use the on-site phone to take advice from the signalling staff. They will ask you how many are in the party and advise when it may be safe to cross. They don't ask you to report after crossing, but if you are alone it may be sensible if you can agree to report that you have successfully crossed. There are phones on both sides of the track.

Having successfully crossed the track go left and immediately right and assess the situation ahead. If the field looks dry, go just to the right of all the silos where a series of gates leads through to the A1. Then follow the Belford Barn straight ahead into the village. When I walked this section, in mid-summer, the path, which passes to the right of the many giant grain silos ahead, was several feet deep in water. The field behind the silos had become very popular with a substantial mallard population. If this is the case, and you have got this far, turn left along the right of way that runs through to the road, parallel with the former goods yard boundary, past a silo inscribed 'Coastal Grains'.

Turn right onto the road and follow the pavement alongside it past the

ambulance station. When you get to the A1, whether you are following the path past the silos Z or the pavement of the B1342 road, take care crossing. Cars in each direction are coming round a curve, and in spite of the best efforts of the local police force, some are definitely approaching at the same speed as the trains just mentioned. Taking that into account, continue the short distance into Belford. Belford has friendly and helpful shops and pubs, accommodation and a mediaeval church.

THE ALTERNATIVE ROUTE:
Seahouses to Bamburgh by the beach

This route will take you along a beautiful sandy beach to Bamburgh via the historic Monks' House referred to in the previous chapter. From Seahouses, come away from the harbour, turn right (north) along the pavement by the road towards Bamburgh Castle, which you can see up the beach. As soon as you are past the car park walk along one of the paths along the cliff top until the sand starts. Make sure the tide is on the way out and keep walking until you reach the Bamburgh Castle. There are good views of the Farnes from the top, a magnificent Edwardian Great Hall, some nice pictures and knights in armour, and it is worth every penny of the entrance fee. Go along the path inland through the dunes from the beach on the southern side of the castle and up to the entrance. I can also recommend lingering a while to visit Bamburgh village, with its pubs, teashops, Grace Darling Museum and magnificent views of the castle.

THE ALTERNATIVE ROUTE:
Bamburgh to Budle on the beaches and cliff tops

This follows the beaches and cliff-top paths to Budle bus stop X on page 117 and then involves a pleasant bus trip to Fenwick or Beale. Get on the top deck in the front seats and enjoy the glimpses of Lindisfarne and its castle in comfort.

To start the walk go either side of Bamburgh Castle onto the beach and go north. Join the road that goes past the lighthouse until you get to the Bamburgh Castle Golf Club. If the tide is too high, which is very rare, walk up through the village away from the castle and take the first turning right. Then follow the road to the Royal Bamburgh Golf Club.

The path through the golf club is clearly marked and a pleasure to walk. You may decide to stay on the path for this stretch if the mood takes you, however, you can walk along the beach here, subject to tides, but you will have to scramble over some rocks for a short part of the way.

Whether you decide to walk along the beach or through the golf course you will come to a pier. Shortly after the pier you will see a wide path through the dunes, which you can use to go on to the cliff top. Alternatively continue along the cliff top (or along

the beach) to the next track going inland and go up that track to Budle. Here there is a bus stop and I would strongly advise timing this to catch the Coast and Castles bus either to Belford, Fenwick or Beal, preferably one of the last two, for your onward journey to Lindisfarne. If you catch the Coast and Castles bus at Budle X, after walking through the Bamburgh Castle Golf Club or the beach, you can get off at Fenwick.

Fenwick Granary is down a lane just south of the bus stop on the A1. From here you can walk to Lindisfarne, having checked the causeway crossing times. Alternatively, continue to Beal on the bus, and walk or take a bus to the island. There is an off-road cycleway/walkway from the A1 bus stop at Beale to the causeway. You could also make an arrangement with a local taxi driver to collect you at this point and drive you on.

If you do this alternative route you can have more time on Lindisfarne. A two-night stay or an all-day visit should give you time to study Lindisfarne Castle (National Trust), the Priory (English Heritage), the fascinating locally run Heritage Centre and the superb National Nature Reserve (Natural England). On the north shores of Lindisfarne, where few venture, there are flower-bedecked dunes, wild cliffs, lots of (very noisy) seals and some archaeological and geological interest thrown in for good measure. All of which is described in Chapter 10.

You will only need to read the first part of this chapter if you have opted for the more challenging, inland, section of the official Northumberland Coast Path. If you have opted to catch the bus from Budle, north of which there is (at the time of writing) no coastal right of way until near the Lindisfarne Causeway, skip to the 'Fenwick to Lindisfarne' section at the end of this chapter. The one saving grace of the inland route here is that you get good glimpses of Lindisfarne, and when you are looking back inland from the island you will recognise the hills. At this stage you may feel it was worth the sweat and mud.

Belford to Fenwick

From the centre of Belford **A** follow the Wooler road sign past the Co-operative food store, the chip shop, the chemist and the Belford Community Club. Take the first turning right down a country lane until you see a kissing gate on your left. There is a wooden sign inscribed 'Public Footpath' and 'Swinhoe 1¾', along with the North Sea Trail symbols. Go through the kissing gate and along the path by a stream, the Belford Burn.

This brings you into an open field with a view of Westhall **B**, a crenellated farmhouse built in 1837 to look like a small castle. The existence of a moat and other earthworks has led to the theory that this is the site of Belford Castle, which is referred to in a number of ancient documents. It is also believed that this is the site of a

15th-century pele tower. Possibly the 19th-century builders of the structure used the stone, since a pele tower no longer seems to exist, unless it is hidden within the structure.

Keep left along the field edge and straight on through the kissing gate, which is simply marked with a public footpath yellow arrow. The stones you are now walking on form the top of a mill dam that used to be here. During work on the dam a mediaeval spur was found. At the end of the field go through another kissing gate and turn right. It can be rather soggy in this corner of the field.

Here you come onto a track with a hedge on your right. You can see the line of the path straight on up onto the horizon ahead of you. You have to cross another stream at Soldier's Dean

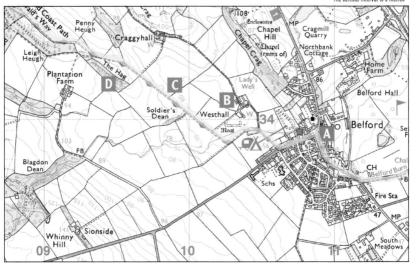

C. There is no footbridge and unless you're wearing wellies, the water could well come over the top of your walking boots and the path can be quite overgrown here. Keep straight on over a wall, straight on up the hill, with a wall on your right. Where this wall goes off to the right and a farm track also forks right just afterwards, take the left-hand fork up to the ridge of the hill (the Hag D). On the ridge you meet another wall. Keep that on your right and cross some mounds ahead of you. Below you to the south-west is Plantation Farm to which a stile leads, but you want to keep going north-west along the top of the ridge. Go through a kissing gate and stay in the fields, keeping the rough area marked as woodland on the map on your left.

Keep going along the ridge until you see a field ahead of you (also marked as woodland on the map) with some large mounds or rock outcrops in it. Cross this field diagonally to the far left-hand corner. Here there is a gate giving access to a farm track. Swinhoe Farm E is an equine centre and there are horse-exercising areas to your right.

Go straight ahead along the farm track with the working buildings on your left and the farm cottages on your right. Then continue straight on. Along the open track here you may come across a small colony of ringlet butterflies with their distinctive eye-like dots. Further along, the track forks as you come into the woods. You fork left and go through the edge of the woods just below Lower Swinhoe Lake.

A Ringlet butterfly.

Belford to Lindisfarne

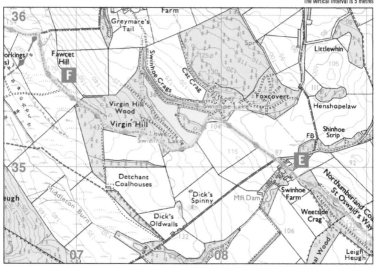

The track through the woods is clear and curves round to go north-west. Keep straight on along the track in the same direction up the hill. As you come out of the woods, still keeping straight on, keep on the level, just to the left of the rocky outcrop of Fawcet Hill F. At the time of writing there were large anti-wind farm signs proclaiming a preference for nuclear power.

Four hundred yards (365 metres) out of the woods you come to the junction of several tracks, the one on the left going south-west being the St Cuthbert's Way. It is signed for St Cuthbert's Cave, which is a 10 to 15-minute walk in each direction if you care for a diversion at this point.

Back at the junction on Fawcet Hill just mentioned, you turn left along a well-made track, which takes you into another forestry plantation, Shiellow Wood. After entering the forest,

fork right and keep going along a nice forest track until it comes to a T-junction, G where a narrow and just about discernible path goes down over a stream and back up again to meet another forest track. This takes you out of the woods once more. Around that stream the path is not very well defined and the ground can be very soft. But keep straight on, follow the forest track and you should come out on Buckton Moor in the corner of a large field H. You will see a permissive path going right: this earthwork is marked as an enclosure on the map I. Our route, however, continues along the forest edge, keeping the forest to your left for nearly a mile. There is another sign indicating another enclosure to the right.

In most parts of England these earthworks could safely be ascribed to the prehistoric age, and archaeological finds show that man was present in this area at the time. However, in this border area, people were also defending themselves in short-term, hurriedly thrown-up enclosures and temporary buildings. This type of activity continued right up to the union with Scotland so not every earthwork can be assumed to be Iron or Bronze Age.

As a matter of interest there is a small hummock marked on the map as Barty's Law. You will see more places called 'Law' as you go north – it means hill. If it has been raining a lot these fields can be more than ankle-deep in mud. It is hard going so allow extra time and be glad if your footwear is keeping all the mud and water away from your feet.

St Cuthbert.

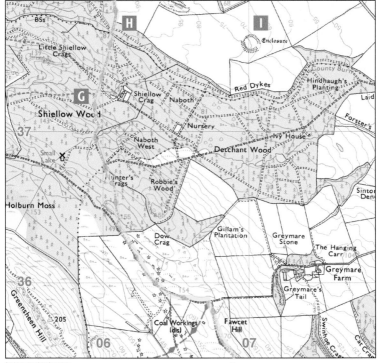

Contours are given in metres
The vertical interval is 5 metres

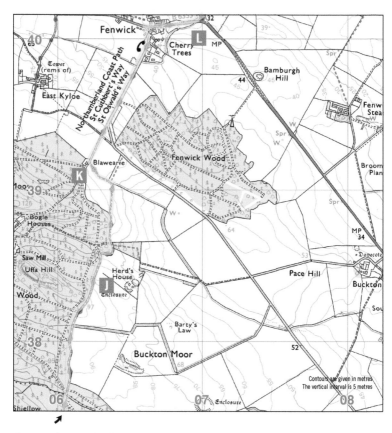

Once you're past the Herd's House earthworks J you go through a small outlier of the forest (particularly muddy), continue along the edge of the forest, and then straight on along the field boundary to the bottom of that field. Turn left into the small field, which borders the forest, and keep along its northern edge until you get to the end of the country lane K. Turn right down the lane and continue into Fenwick.

Fenwick to Lindisfarne

There is a bed and breakfast in Fenwick, and a bus stop on the A1 L. From the junction in the centre of Fenwick go down to the A1. If you have arrived at the bus stop go down the adjacent lane towards the coast. You will pass the rather fine farm buildings of Fenwick Granary M, including a superb dovecote. Continue on down the road until you see a small group of buildings on the right. Turn left here for a footpath along the track, which skirts around a disused quarry N and continues to another road. Turn right along the road and then left along Fishers' Back Road towards the sea. Sadly the road has somehow disappeared but you go down through the field with a hedge on your left until you come to the railway line O. Use the phone to get permission to cross from the signal staff. At least on this crossing you do get quite a good view of oncoming trains and so I didn't find it as frightening as the Belford Station crossing.

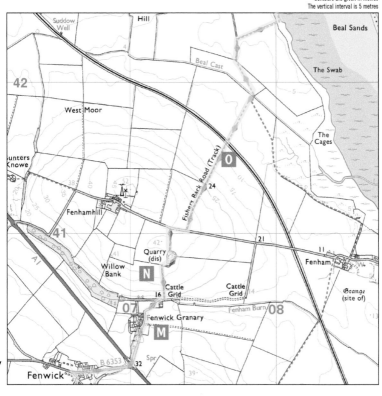

Contours are given in metres
The vertical interval is 5 metres

Lindisfarne Castle is now in sight.

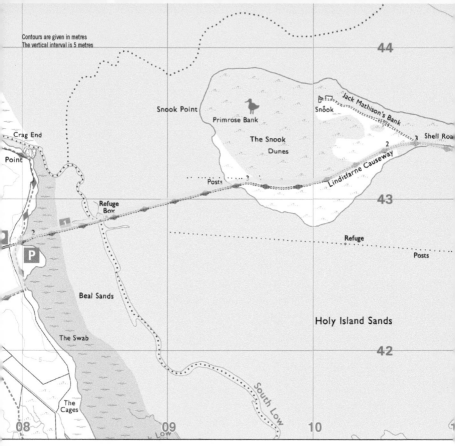

Contours are given in metres
The vertical interval is 5 metres

44

Snook Point

Primrose Bank

Jack Mathison's Bank

Snook

Crag End

The Snook

Dunes

Shell Roa

Point

3

Lindisfarne Causeway

2

Posts

3

43

Refuge
Box

2

Refuge

Posts

P

Beal Sands

Holy Island Sands

The Swab

42

5

The
Cages

South Low

08

09

10

w Low

Dark green fritillary on the Lindisfarne dunes.

Keep straight on after the railway, cross a small stream, the Beal Cast, and turn diagonally left across the field. Then follow the track briefly north and turn right down to the Beal Sands P.

When you reach the coast there is a line of familiar dragon's teeth Second World War defensive blocks. Turn left and north until you reach the causeway. There is a car park here along with some information signs. Make absolutely sure before you reach this point that you have timed your arrival to be well within the open times for the causeway. The times are posted here but you could have a very long wait indeed if you don't look them up online or make enquiries locally beforehand.

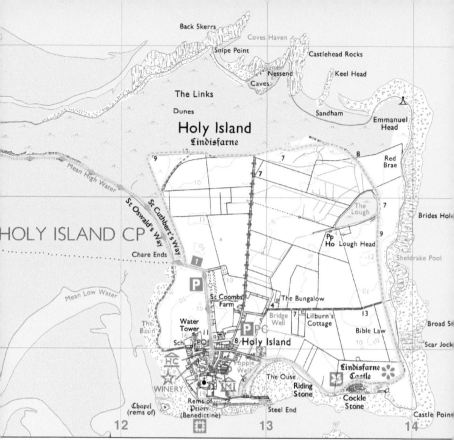

Follow the road across the causeway. The posts that mark the old pilgrim's route are used on ceremonial occasions. It is not advisable for people who have no local knowledge to follow that route, so it is best to keep close to the road all the way. From the mainland to the village is about 3 miles (5 km) so allow at least an hour for brisk walking or a couple of hours if you want to take your time, take some photos, watch the wading birds and identify some of the plants along the way.

Chapter 10 will describe the delights of the Holy Island of Lindisfarne, the priory, the castle, and its beautiful and rare wildlife.

Refuge on the causeway for those that get caught by the tides.

10 Holy Island

Round walk through Lindisfarne National Nature Reserve including Green Shiel, Castlehead Rocks and Coves Haven

4.2 miles (6.8 km)

You cannot say you have walked the whole Northumberland coast without walking around this island. The landscape and wildlife are extraordinary and the walking easy. The historical interest is among the top features of Northumberland: Anglo-Saxon England, mediaeval Europe and Norman Britain. To top all that, in the early 20th century some coastal fortifications were transformed into one of the most photographed castles in the country. The renovation was by Edwin

Lutyens (the architect who designed New Delhi) and a garden created by Gertrude Jekyll, which the National Trust recreated and maintains with great pride.

Most of the 500,000 visitors who come here every year visit for a few hours at most, enjoy a drink or a meal in one of the cafés or pubs and go away again. There really is enough here to spend several days enjoying the walks, the ruins, the seals and the flowers, not to mention hospitality. You will not regret having spent extra time here and you may want to return again. If you are staying overnight I should just warn you about the roaring seals. As the tide comes in and squeezes them all onto narrower spaces on the rocks and sands around the island, this strange and wonderful sound can briefly interrupt your sleep. But you do get used to it, and it will be one of the many memories of your stay. As this is a book about walking the coast I shall describe the walk around Lindisfarne Island's coast first.

From the village car park **A**, go back along the road towards the causeway to the bend in the road, which is next

Rocky shore and cliffs at Coves Haven.

View showing the basalt (whin sill) foundations of this imposing fort, as well as part of Lutyen's additions.

to the south-western end of the car park. There is a wooden sign on that corner pointing north-west. The path leads across a fairly flat area of dunes just outside the field boundaries. Keep going north and straight on into the dunes. You should see remains of some old limekilns in the dunes B. Go to the right of these and keep going north and you should come across Green Shiel C. There is a small information board explaining that the buildings found during an excavation carried out by Leeds University are probably farm buildings of the Anglo-Saxon period. They surmise that such buildings would have been related to the raising of cattle. The Anglo-Saxon Lindisfarne Monastery (AD 634–875), famous for its scribes, would have needed the highest quality calfskins to make the parchment for the documents. Therefore it is quite possible that the documents (realistic electronic copies of which you will see in the Lindisfarne Heritage Centre HC) originated from the spot. We know little else about what lies below these dunes, which were formed in relatively recent times. The nature reserve site staff ask you to keep to existing paths around the dunes to minimise disturbance and contact with the invasive weed pirr-pirri, which is present throughout the dunes.

Having taken in this information at Green Shiel you can continue on to the beach at Snipe Point D. You will also see quite a few gannets fishing off the coast here. Look out for something rather whiter and larger than a herring gull. At a distance it is the white flashes in the sunlight that most attract the eye to them. They dive from 100 feet (39 metres) and hit the water at up to 70 mph (110 kph). There is a large colony on Bass Rock, which you will see from St Abb's Head. Their numbers have been increasing in recent years and this is mainly thanks to careful management of the nesting grounds at Bass Rock.

An additional reason is that 'bycatch', the system of throwing fish back into the sea to comply with current European fishing regulations, means that the gannets have learnt to visit the trawler fleets to take up the surplus fish. This was discovered when research on Bass Rock showed that the gannets were bringing in fish that live much deeper than the 65-foot (20-metre) depth to which they can dive. You can also go up to Bass Rock for a close-up view if you visit North Berwick harbour and take one of the boat trips offered there during the nesting season. When I visited, there were also very large numbers of grey seals on the rocks, along with oystercatchers and ringed plovers running around on the beach and in the rocks. Here at Coves Haven E there are cliffs and a rocky beach backed by floral displays in a duneland nature reserve. Butterflies feed on the flowers and in between the dunes you catch glimpses of the fantastic castle to the south.

Most people who visit this piece of Northumberland's coast have no idea that this cove exists. It's a particularly wonderful place in the (still) secret Kingdom of Northumbria. If you are there at dawn or dusk you may see the barn owl swooping across the reserve and neighbouring fields. Late one evening when I was there, a lone osprey

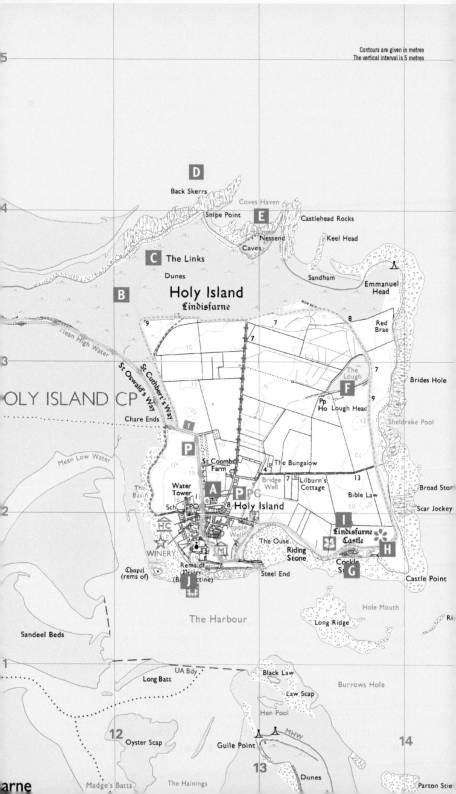

Contours are given in metres
The vertical interval is 5 metres

5

D

Back Skerrs

Coves Haven

4

Snipe Point

E

Castlehead Rocks

Nessend

Keel Head

Caves

C The Links

Dunes

Sandham

Emmanuel
Head

B

Holy Island
Lindisfarne

9

7

8

Red
Brae

Mean High Water

7

7

3

The Lough

7

F

Brides Hole

St Cuthbert's Way

St Oswald's Way

OLY ISLAND CP

Pp
Ho Lough Head

9

Chare Ends

Sheldrake Pool

1

P

-12

Mean Low Water

St Coombs
Farm

The Bungalow

4

Bridge
Well

7

Lilburn's
Cottage

13

A

P

Water
Tower

Sch

PO

Holy Island

Bible Law

10

I

Broad Stor

The
Basin

HC

Popple
Well

**Lindisfarne
Castle**

Scar Jockey

H

WINERY

Rems of
Priory
(Benedictine)

J

The Ouse

Riding
Stone

Cockle
S

G

Castle Point

Steel End

2

Hole Mouth

The Harbour

Long Ridge

Ri

Sandeel Beds

1

UA Bdy

Black Law

Burrows Hole

Long Batt

Law Scap

Hen Pool

12

Oyster Scap

Guile Point

MHW

14

13

Dunes

Parton Stie

arne

Madge's Batts

The Hainings

Inverted boats used for storage, looking across the bay to Lindisfarne Castle.

was gliding very high over the reserve.

On the way back you will pass the Lough F, a large pond with an excellent hide next to it. It may have been excavated by the monks as a fish pond and fresh water supply. Have binoculars at the ready to spot what's there. You may be able to get a copy of the excellent *Natural England Lindisfarne National Nature Reserve* leaflet, usually available from the car parks, reserve hides and tourist information centres. The leaflet is also available on the Natural England website and can be downloaded in PDF format, or read from your smartphone or tablet. It includes detailed information on what to look for in the reserve and a nature trail that approximately follows the route suggested here.

Using the castle G as your guiding landmark, I would suggest that you return close to the eastern coast of Lindisfarne on the track bed of the 19th-century railway, which took limestone from this part of the island. Go south and then south-east away from Coves Haven on one of the tracks through the dunes. See if you can identify the limestone quarries, which supplied the gigantic limekilns by the Lindisfarne Castle. Some of the higher dunes have completely hidden the old railway here, but if you go slightly left of the direction of the castle you will see the path, which runs along the southern boundary of the reserve. Join that path and turn left when you reach it. Soon the old railway track becomes apparent and you follow it, curving right all the way to Lindisfarne Castle.

After the dissolution of the monasteries by Henry VIII a fort was built in the mid-16th century using stone from the then unoccupied monastery. This fort served until the 19th century as barracks, a small outpost for the British Army watching the eastern shores. There was accommodation there, separate buildings that contained explosives, and a vegetable patch which helped to supplement the soldiers' food supplies. The position of the fort overlooking the last deep-water harbour before you reach the Scottish border was an important factor in its defensive role during the 300 years it was occupied. The soldiers left in 1893.

In the 20th century the editor of *Country Life* magazine, Edward Hudson, bought the castle and invited the architect Edwin Lutyens and the landscape architect Gertrude Jekyll to remodel the barrack buildings and the soldiers' vegetable plot. This site was then to serve as the setting for quite an unusual country home for an Edwardian London-based editor with an equally unusual garden 500 yards (460 metres) to the north. In 1944 Lindisfarne Castle and the area around it was given to the National Trust. In season the castle is closed on Mondays and opening times depend on the tides. National Trust members will of course have free entry. In winter the castle is open on certain published dates. See their website, excellent smartphone app, or handbook to find the dates.

The austere external appearance of Lindisfarne Castle has been made famous worldwide by paintings and prize-winning photographs. A visit to the interior is an absolute must. The first thing you will see as you go up to the castle are the inverted boats serving as storerooms. Lutyens saw the inverted boats being used by the fishermen in the bay, as they still are, and decided to incorporate some in his new design. On entry to the Castle you'll see a recently purchased,

magnificent oil painting of this castle in moonlight. This shows it as it would have been at the time when the limekilns were active and glowing all night. The moon is reflected in the bay, and the castle shows as a grand outline against the rising moon.

On your right is a painted panel 8 feet (2.5 metres) across showing the escaping Spanish Armada, the many castles of the Northumberland coast, and the island of Lindisfarne. If you visited the castle a decade or so ago you may not have noticed this. The panel had become darkened by age and had little of its original impact. Now the panel, originally painted by an artist called MacDonald Gill, has been painstakingly cleaned by expert restorer Jim Devenport and can be seen in all its original glory. The panel incorporates a wind-direction indicator, which has also been restored and is still working. This device was originally installed one century ago.

A leaflet will be given to you on entry describing all the different rooms

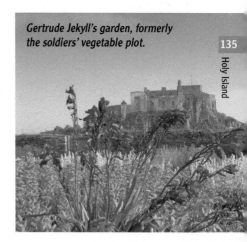

Gertrude Jekyll's garden, formerly the soldiers' vegetable plot.

The castle dining room.

and the layout of the castle as it is now and as it was as barracks. As I walked around the interior, I found it quite interesting trying to work out the changes that Lutyens had made. The dining room particularly caught my attention. The dark blue of the dining room west wall is a feature of the Lutyens conversion, the dining table was designed by Lutyens, and you can still find a small bread oven in the north-east corner. As you come out onto the upper battery, designed to attack any enemy boats trying to gain access to the harbour, you get superb views of places where you have recently walked, and where you will be going if you complete the walk described in this book.

To the north, on a clear day, you can see the lighthouse at St Abb's Head in Berwickshire, Scotland. If you complete the walk this is the northern limit of your visit to this coast. Originally this was also close to the northern limit of the Anglo-Saxon Kingdom of Northumberland. To the left of the lighthouse is Berwick-upon-Tweed. Looking straight out to sea is the Longstone Lighthouse which you may

have visited if you spent a little extra time in Seahouses, which you can also make out when it is clear enough.
To the right of Longstone are, from left to right, Brownsman Island with its old light, Staple Island and Inner Farne with its white lighthouse. To the south you can also see the navigation beacons on Ross Sands and Bamburgh Castle. The beacons can be lined up by skippers coming into the harbour here to enable safe entry. To fully appreciate this view you must have walked past the places that you can see from this point. It must count as one of the most memorable viewpoints of outstanding landmarks anywhere in Europe.

That the authorities have managed to keep this a secret from international visitors for so long is an outstanding British achievement of the 20th and 21st centuries. As you leave the castle be sure, if you have not already done so, to visit the limekilns H. From the castle you will come to the top part of the structure, where the lime and coal was tipped into the kilns from above. The railway track that you will have walked down as part of your visit to the nature reserve led from the limestone quarries to these kilns. The wagons were horse-drawn but the final few yards involved just the men who had to push the wagons to the fiery tops of the kilns. The horses intensely disliked going so close to the heat. The coal was brought from Northumbrian coal mines along this coast. As you go along the Coast Path note the word 'shafts', which invariably marks the sites of former coal mines.

There are older limekilns **B** that you will have seen on your walk to the north-western corner of the island, near Green Shiels. However, these industrial-scale limekilns by the castle were built in the 1860s by William Nicoll, a Dundee businessman, and operated until the turn of the 20th century. It is worth going down now to sea level and exploring inside the kilns.

The next place to go is Gertrude Jekyll's garden **I**. There are fine views looking back to the Lindisfarne Castle, and in 2002 the National Trust began to restore Jekyll's original plan. Return to the village around the bay. The views of the castle change constantly according to the weather, the time of day and the angle of view.

I suggest that you next visit the priory **J**. This, like the castle, is signed with traditional cast-iron signs. Some people object to paying the English Heritage fee to go into the abbey and sneak a look from the parish graveyard. If you do this you will be missing a

great deal. First of all, when you pay your entrance fee, or use your English Heritage membership to go in, you will see the display of how the priory might have looked over the millennia that the religion of Christianity has influenced the appearance of this island.

The earliest part of the story is that King Oswald, whose family had been thrown out of the area at an earlier date, was educated at Iona, now part of Scotland, then part of Ireland, where the Celtic church had been converting people to Christianity for some time.

Oswald ruled the united Kingdom of Northumberland, consisting of Bernicia and Deira, and stretching from the Humber to the Firth of Forth. His base was Bamburgh Castle. When Oswald regained power in AD 633 he recruited the monk Aidan from Iona to work on converting the local population to Christianity and gave him the Island of Lindisfarne for the establishment of the early Anglo-Saxon monastery. This would have been a wooden structure

Be sure to go inside the castle to see the painting with the limekilns glowing in moonlight.

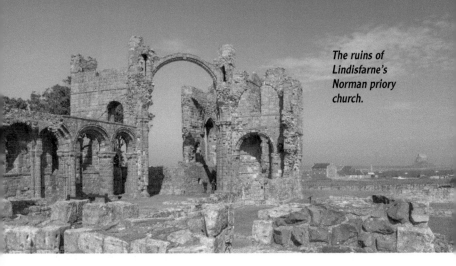

The ruins of Lindisfarne's Norman priory church.

and no trace remains, although objects from it have been found. The monk Cuthbert, who some time later also worked hard to convert the local population, eventually became Bishop of Lindisfarne (the Irish church based its bishops in the country, not in the cities). Both Aidan and Cuthbert used Inner Farne Island as a base for seclusion as hermits, sometimes for Lent and sometimes for longer periods. Another monk called Bede, who would have been 14 years old when Cuthbert died, immortalised the history of this period and is regarded as a reliable historical source to this day. He even recorded the dates accurately of numerous events at this time. Cuthbert died on Inner Farne on 20 March 687. Over 100 churches in England are dedicated to St Cuthbert. Oswald also became a saint and has churches dedicated to him as far afield as Hildesheim in Germany, and in Prague.

Whether you are religious or not, the history of Anglo-Saxon civilisation in this outpost on the edge of the known world is quite remarkable. The establishment founded by the Norman kings on this site can still be seen, and the English Heritage display shows how this came to be.

Having taken in as much of the English Heritage exhibition as you can, visit the abbey ruins. First of all look down the full length of the nave. The transverse archway that you see is all that remains of the tower crossing. But look closely at the Norman columns to the left and you will see the typical chevron and other designs used in the mother Abbey, now the Cathedral, of Durham.

If you have studied the layout of the rest of the site carefully you will see that this is no typical monastic settlement. The buildings to the coastal side of Lindisfarne Abbey were laid out more in the style of a country residence of the time than a typical monastery. In addition, you can see the crenellated wall showing that it was, like Tynemouth, defended quite strongly. It is worth referring to the English Heritage publication *Lindisfarne Priory* to see how the site would have looked in the past and to get a clear idea of the significance of this site in the history of England. The next place to visit is the Lindisfarne Heritage Centre

HC, which may clarify many of the aspects of your visit by filling in the details of much that you have seen during your visit so far. Having spent some time in the centre you may well decide to revisit some of the sites again with this additional understanding.

I shall give a brief description of the complex circumstances leading to the establishment of a religious settlement on Lindisfarne later. Once at Lindisfarne there are several very good exhibitions, in particular in the Heritage Centre, which give an excellent explanation of the extraordinary circumstances leading to the production of major works of art, using materials from throughout the known world and very highly skilled people to carry out the work. We are only just beginning to become aware of all this. These works are the Lindisfarne Gospels. There is a facsimile of the work in Lindisfarne Heritage Centre with a very comprehensive explanation of its creation.

The unique factor in the centre is the electronic display of the *Anglo-Saxon Lindisfarne Gospels.* The book, which was produced on this island over one millennium ago, is still in existence through an extraordinary sequence of events, about which you can learn more at the centre. The book is now in the possession of the British Library, and is due to spend alternate years in there and in Durham Cathedral, so that it may be viewed locally as well as internationally in alternate years.

You do not need to follow any particular faith to be able to understand the significance of the production of this document. What is extraordinary, apart from the fact that the written material still exists and is in good condition, is that, if you learnt Latin at school, you will still be able to read every word that was written so long ago, since it is written in Latin script very similar to the one we use today.

Its significance in world history may lead to a greater understanding if you study the objects and texts displayed in this centre. Careful study of the exhibits will reveal many fascinating and little-known facts about the advanced world trade routes and sophistication of these early times in our history.

During my first visits to the island I was unaware of the existence of the Lindisfarne Heritage Centre at the western end of the village. The signs are entirely separate from the traditional cast-iron signs to the cathedral and castle, and are posted on walls in a Celtic script that might lead you to believe that they are advertising for one of the island's commercial outlets, cafés or pubs. Let me assure you that this locally sponsored and created exhibition is well worth the entry fee. It will explain nearly every facet of the historical, botanical, biological and scenic aspect of the island and enrich your visit no end. It is quite separate from, but complementary to, the English Heritage displays by the priory. Try to find time to visit both.

Near the Heritage Centre is a small garden with a cross where visitors may care to take a rest and absorb all that they have experienced on this island.

Lindisfarne to St Abbs

Day 1 Lindisfarne to Berwick-upon-Tweed
13.8 miles (22.2 km)

Day 2 Berwick-upon-Tweed
3 miles (4,8 km) but up to 12 miles (19.3 km) depending on how extensive your exploration is

Day 3 Berwick-upon-Tweed to St Abbs
14.7 miles (23.5 km), plus 3.6 miles (6 km) for St Abb's Head

From Lindisfarne to Berwick-upon-Tweed

This is a good day's walking. The path is variable, but the sand dune nature reserves are stunning in spring and summer, and the rock formations are as dramatic as they come. Do note that as you approach Berwick-upon-Tweed, you should keep on the cliff top as people do get trapped by incoming tides if they get distracted on the beaches. The walk is marginally more strenuous than at points south of this, but an early start will ensure a timely arrival at Berwick-upon-Tweed, which has lots of good reasonably priced accommodation and the best town ramparts in northern Europe.

From Berwick-upon-Tweed to St Abbs

I can heartily recommend this walk. The Scottish stretch is well surfaced and maintained with comprehensive signing, bridges over the streams, legible waymarks, a complete change of surroundings and superb cliff scenery.

This chapter briefly covers the path north of Berwick, since the first stretch is still in England, and has a few scenic surprises as well as more flowers and birds to see. The English stretch stops on a cliff top by a railway line, so there are very brief instructions on how to get to St Abb's Head, from which you can see Bass Rock, home of the gannets you have been seeing out at sea much of the way up from the south. St Abb's Head and St Abbs itself, is a lovely little fishing harbour where you can

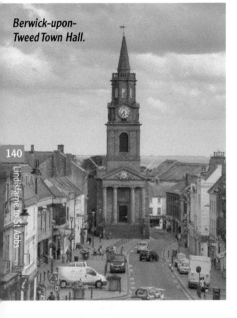
Berwick-upon-Tweed Town Hall.

sit and enjoy refreshments on licensed premises, and congratulate yourself on completing an international walk.

The whole route is linked with good bus services from morning to mid-afternoon, and this applies to links between St Abbs and Berwick if you decide to extend your walk up to and beyond the Scottish border.

Day 1 Lindisfarne to Berwick-upon-Tweed

The best time to start from Lindisfarne is on a falling tide after the causeway is opened. This gives you plenty of time to cross the causeway (allow at least an hour) and to tackle the first ¾ mile (1 km) going north which is more or less on the beach. Having crossed the Lindisfarne Causeway turn right

along the back of the beach. It is quite lumpy walking but there are some interesting plants along the way. On reaching Beal Point **A** the path turns left and inland to keep just outside the fence up to Longbridge End **B**. It is not a very distinct path and the area is a little marshy but you are on the right track. At 600 yards (550 metres) inland from Beal Point you will meet a well-surfaced track, which is National Cycle Route 1. If you are starting from Beal, from the bus stop on the A1, you can use the cycleway, which is separate from the road all the way to this point.

As you join the cycleway turn right and north over a short causeway and bridge. After going over the bridge the path bears right and then left onto softer marshy land. You may see cyclists with retired road bikes carrying their bicycles over this section. Up ahead

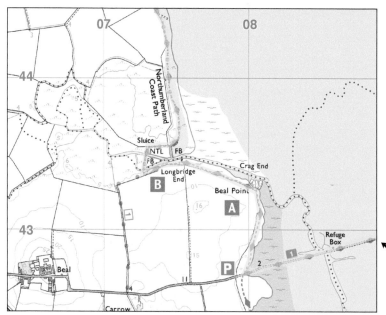

Contours are given in metres
The vertical interval is 5 metres

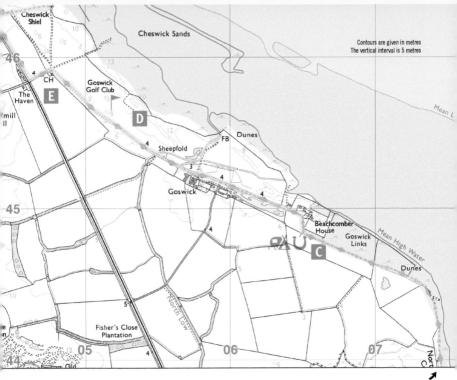

you will see a wartime outlook tower C and a small group of white-gabled buildings to the left of it. Go through the kissing gate and keep straight on and you come to a track. As you continue north you come to Goswick Links, Goswick (the small group of buildings just beyond the lake on the left) and Goswick Golf Club D. Look inland and you will catch sight of the distinctive tower at Haggerston Castle.

Goswick was identified at the beginning of the Second World War as one of the places in Britain where a landing was likely in the case of an invasion. The beach would have been an easy landing place. A good rail link was within yards. The railway could have been used for a massive tank advance to start with and then used to transport large numbers of troops and equipment into the heart of England. To deter the enemy, the beach and

coastline here was provided with extra reinforcement against attack. Landmines were laid on the beaches here and extra concrete tank traps installed. Vehicle obstacles, pillboxes and machine gun emplacements, along with anti-glider poles and an observation tower were all installed during the Second World War. Once the threat of invasion was realised to be less likely, following the breaking of the codes by Intelligence, the area was used for training aircraft crews to drop bombs before they went into live action. You will see that quite a lot of the evidence for all this activity is still visible. Between 1945 and the end of the 20th century bomb disposal squads combed the area and regularly blew up unexploded ordnance.

The Goswick Golf Course clubhouse E has a sign welcoming walkers. It could

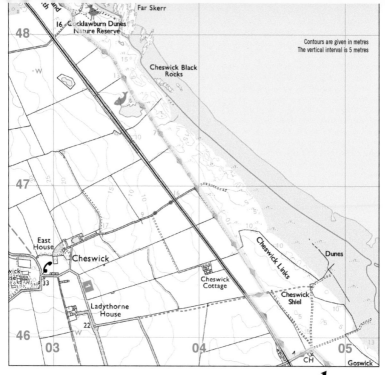

well be that a cup of tea or a snack would be welcome at this stage. From the clubhouse follow the road inland from the golf club and you'll see a sign pointing right, north, just before the railway crossing. The path currently goes to the far end of the practice area, turns right away from the railway line towards the sea to the corner of a couple of fields. Here you will find the kissing gate with the North Sea Trail waymark pointing left. This indicates that the path goes up onto the bank where you turn right and continue straight on to another kissing gate. This part of the path can be unpleasantly overgrown. Once you go through this last kissing gate the fields are grazed by cattle and make an easy walk across the turf.

There are plans to take the cycleway on the shorter route at Goswick golf course, possibly through here. If that has happened when you get here life

may be easier. Keep straight on and you come to the last outpost of the Lindisfarne National Nature Reserve. There is a good information panel at the entrance to the reserve, where you rejoin the cycleway. From here to Berwick you can follow the cycleway signs the whole way to Spittal, where you can scramble down a path to the promenade.

From here to Berwick the North Sea Trail will be going north-west on a track or road. If there is a single fence then the path is outside it. Where you follow the railway line into Berwick-upon-Tweed the path runs parallel with the wall along the railway line.

Returning to the spot where we are now, this is the Cocklawburn Dunes Nature Reserve F. Once again the flowers in the dunes here are magnificent. Photographers – make

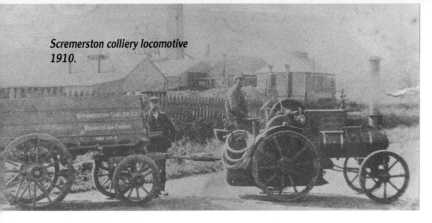

Scremerston colliery locomotive 1910.

sure you still have space on your memory card to record some of these wonderful plants. Allow some time to have a look around if you have an interest in these scenes.

As you leave the reserve the track becomes a road and after a few hundred yards there is a small car park. At the end of Cocklawburn ('ck' not pronounced) Beach you'll see that Saltpan How and Saltpan Rocks G are on the map. Boiling sea water

in pans for salt, using the local coal, was a major economic activity all the way along the Northumberland coast, hence the word 'pan' featuring in many place names.

You are now in the parish of Scremerston. Note from the map the place name Borewell and the disused mines, shafts and pits, as well as the dismantled railway line, all giving the clue that until quite recent times (1944) this was a coal-mining area.

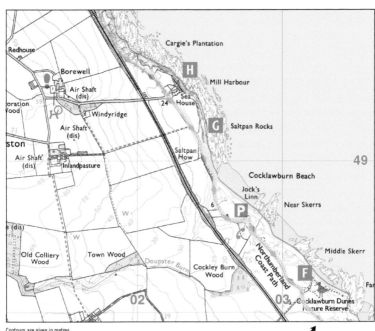

Contours are given in metres
The vertical interval is 5 metres

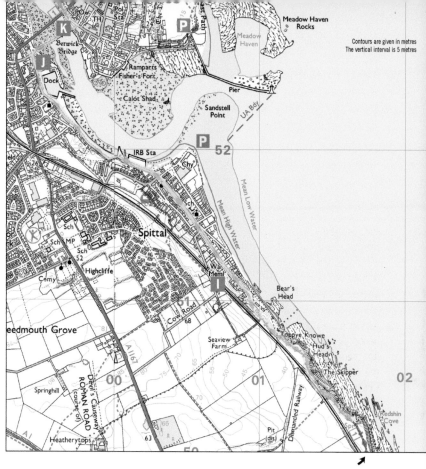

Contours are given in metres
The vertical interval is 5 metres

In addition, the geological formations here are much studied. The contorted shapes are a good indication of the massive movements which took place here millions of years ago. Fossils are also found here, and the Great North Museum in Newcastle has on display a giant fish that was found in recent years. If you are interested in geology, a visit to the Great North Museum would be worthwhile.

After Saltpan Rocks you'll see a prominent, long house perpendicular to the cliff H. The road here goes left and inland but the path goes straight ahead along the track and then into some very muddy fields.

When you get into Spittal you'll see a small path going down to the promenade. Buses go from the war memorial I just back from the promenade. At the time of writing the last bus was at 10pm.

If you are going to do this walk properly, continue along the promenade until you see a tall chimney on your left enclosed behind a high wall. Go around the headland here and along the beach, or the road. Now go onto the pavement along the road on the southern bank of the River Tweed. Keep going past the docks J, staying on the level, and take the first turning right, which brings you into

Berwick-upon-Tweed Town Hall left, and the stone bridge built at the beginning of the reign of James I of England, by royal command, to replace the wooden structure not fit for a king.

Berwick-upon-Tweed over the ancient mediaeval Berwick Bridge K.

If you are looking for the youth hostel L turn right immediately after crossing the bridge. The hostel is an old granary building just behind the wall a few yards from the bridge. It can be accessed through a small gate in the wall from the harbour edge or from the wall itself. Presumably for conservation reasons it is not clearly marked but you should find it if you follow these instructions. In the same building there are quite often excellent exhibitions of one sort or another, particularly during the winter period when the barracks are closed to the public.

If you plan to base yourself in Berwick it can be a good idea to be near the railway station, which is where the buses to other parts of the walk start and finish. It is also close to the old castle remains, the Royal Border Bridge and a short walk from the walls.

If you need to leave luggage near the station (they have no left-luggage facilities) the Tweed View Guest House and Bed and Breakfast by the station entrance will take luggage in return for a suitable charity donation.

Day 2 Berwick-upon-Tweed

This book is about walking the Coast Path but it would be a great pity not to spend at least a day exploring the Elizabethan ramparts and the mediaeval walls of Berwick-upon-Tweed. The ramparts compare with

some of the best in Italy and were actually designed in conjunction with an Italian military engineer. The costs involved were stupendous and ultimately part of ramparts – the section where the danger of attack was least likely – was not built, but the mediaeval walls were repaired. This is the reason why the walls are virtually complete and can be followed on an excellent path all the way around the town.

If you arrive in the late afternoon or evening I would recommend a quick walk around the entire town just to get your bearings. If you do so I suggest you note where the Berwick-upon-Tweed Barracks M, the Town Centre (TIC) N, the flat-roofed Cromwellian church O and the railway station are located.

The barracks at Berwick-upon-Tweed claim to be the first such buildings to be constructed in Britain following the exit of the Romans. They are administered by English Heritage but contain a Regimental Museum, the history of the Army, a Town Museum and Berwick-upon-Tweed's very own Burrell Collection. The shipping magnate, Sir William Burrell, gave part of his collection to Berwick-upon-Tweed because of his love for the town. The rest, of course, went to Glasgow. There are, however, some gems on display during the April to September

Contours are given in metres
The vertical interval is 5 metres

The southern walls of Berwick-upon-Tweed.

opening times. Out of season they may be on display elsewhere in the town so enquire at the tourist information centre. The Burrell Collection is upstairs in the building facing you as you enter the courtyard. The Town Museum is downstairs. The history of the army and Regimental Museum are on your left.

You may think that you would not be particularly interested in a museum devoted to the British Army, but if you do go in you will be pleasantly surprised. It covers the development of the art of keeping the peace, at least amongst the civilian populations of our country.

This exhibition shows how the attempts by armed members of the forces to produce peace in the streets were found to be no longer fruitful during the civil unrest at the beginning of the 19th century. It also tells you why barracks were built in towns throughout Britain and why the occupants of every town were glad to see the soldiers housed properly, instead of being billeted in private homes.

The ramparts of Berwick-upon-Tweed have excellent historical panels explaining how they were designed to work, how they were built, who built them and when. Having completed the circuit of those ramparts, do not neglect to visit the remains of the mediaeval walls, which were even more extensive. To do this you can go through the Co-operative car park on the outside of the ramparts and turn left along a footpath. Turn left again to see the Bell Tower P.

The mediaeval 'white wall' which defended the banks of the Tweed below Berwick Castle.

This is on the line of the original mediaeval walls, which enclosed a much larger area and joined onto Berwick-upon-Tweed Castle, some of which has survived behind the railway station Q. To see those remains either walk along the river upstream and under the Royal Border railway bridge R. Beyond the railway bridge you can turn right and go up through a small park, coming out behind the railway station. In the Town Museum there is an excellent reconstruction of the castle which Robert Stephenson's railway cut right through. If you studied the castle model in the museum you can still get a very good idea of how it would have looked in its full glory.

Day 3
Berwick-upon-Tweed to St Abbs

To start the walk to St Abbs go along the walls from the mediaeval bridge towards the sea and keep going, possibly going up the steps to the public open space above. Make the cliff top and then follow the cliff north. It's about 3 miles (5 km) to the English border T. The red sandstone cliffs are a complete change from the dunes, which you have been travelling through further south. On the way to St Abb's Head you will pass quite a few golf courses and several caravan sites. The railway line is never far

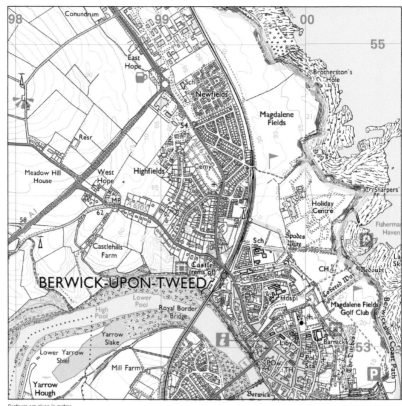

Contours are given in metres
The vertical interval is 5 metres

The arch and stacks of Needles Eye on the coast path, 2 miles (3 km) north of Berwick-upon-Tweed.

away. The trains are travelling at 125 mph (200 kph) but pass every 20 minutes or so surprisingly quietly.

The first remarkable feature you come across, next to a golf course, is a tiny, round bay called Brotherston's Hole. When I was there the golfers seemed to be striking the balls right across the bay. The next feature is the Needles Eye **S**. This is a rock archway with a stack on top of it, indicating a former much higher sea level. There is a colony of auks there from April to July. I saw guillemots and razorbills on the rocks, and I'm told there are one or two puffins hidden up there as well.

Soon after that, you cross the Scottish border **T** and there is a sign welcoming you to Scotland. There is also a border sign on the railway line itself. The path goes inland at the border for the width

of the field and then continues along the seaward side of the road line all the way to Burnmouth.

Approaching Burnmouth you pass a farm **U** and drop down onto the track for access to it. Where this access track turns left under the railway, the path goes right and steeply down the side of the field and then beside

Welcome to Scotland, but no welcome to Northumberland or England coming the other way.

Lindisfarne to St Abbs

a stream. It comes out between the houses at Cowdrait. Turn left along a very attractive harbour and take the road left up to the top of the hill. Turn right by the school and out into the fields along the cliff top all the way to Eyemouth. As you approach Eyemouth Golf Club **W** there is a sign inviting you to follow the cliff top instead of crossing the golf course on the official path down to the harbour. I can heartily recommend following the cliff top as far as you can go. The geological contortions here are absolutely fascinating and the cliffs are wild and beautiful. When you reach Nestsends you will see the road that leads to the lifeboat station and the eastern side of the harbour. Go past the lifeboat station out onto the quay (right) that leads to the end of the harbour. Look out for the harbour seals. Go down the other side of the harbour, along the beach and up onto the cliffs to the seaward side of the caravan site (Corn Fort). From here to St Abbs the path goes along the cliff top and across the beaches here and there, and is well

Lindisfarne to St Abbs

St Abb's Head Lighthouse.

Contours are given in metres
The vertical interval is 5 metres

marked, with bridges over the streams and a good surface all the way.

When you get to St Abbs, visit the centre above the harbour **M** and the National Trust for Scotland information displays **V** below their car park just up the road. Don't miss the walk along the coast to the lighthouse and Pettico Wick, via the lighthouse road. Come back on the tracks to St Abbs. The St

Abb's Head National Nature Reserve is managed by the National Trust for Scotland.

I would like to say a lot more about this but this is the end of the book. If you want to walk on to Edinburgh, follow the John Muir Way along the next piece of coast. I hope you have enjoyed your walk.

PART THREE
USEFUL INFORMATION

Transport

These are services published for 2016. Check online or with the local tourist office for updates. The buses can be useful for focusing your walk on, say, two or three centres of your choice between Newcastle and Berwick and returning to a base each night. The buses can also prove useful when finding a place to stay if everything is full up for that night and you have to get to a vacant B&B somewhere else.

It's a good idea to keep a bus timetable on you in case you don't quite make your destination.

There is also the Metro system that has frequent trains between Newcastle, Tynemouth and Whitley Bay.

Cycling holidays

If you live in one of the world's larger conurbations where buses and suburban trains carry bikes out of rush-hour times, note that none of the local public transport organisations around Tyneside will carry them. National Rail (www.nationalrail.co.uk) services do carry limited numbers. It is advisable to book early as spaces are often limited. This means you will need car support if you want to base yourself at the same location

and use bike routes for parts of the North Sea Trail. Folding bicycles are normally allowed on bus and train services

The Coaster

This is the bus to use if you want to do the southern section of the trail in bite-size bits or if you find a nice place to stay somewhere along its route and decide to use it as a backbone for covering the first 20 miles (32 km). If your plan does not quite work out because you planned to go too far each day or the weather goes seriously downhill, the frequency of this service, and the fact that it runs from early to late every day, means it will come to the rescue.

Coaster buses run every 15 minutes on Monday to Saturday daytimes and every 30 minutes in the evening. Later evening buses will run between Newcastle city centre and North Shields only, but that's within walking distance of Tynemouth anyway.

The Go North East no. 1 service the 'Coaster' starts from Gateshead and stops on the north side of the Tyne Bridge (Gateshead–Newcastle–Byker–Wallsend–North Shields–Tynemouth–Marden–Whitley Bay). Runs every day frequently (four per hour) and is slightly less frequent on Sundays. Get the timetable at www.simplygo.com or get the free app Go North East on your smartphone/pad. This locates your nearest bus stop on the ground, and tells you when the next bus is due. It is also meant to tell you where it is if it is late.

The Arriva bus 308 can come to the rescue if you end up in or near Blyth and need to get back to Whitley Bay or Newcastle. It starts from Newcastle's Haymarket bus station and serves Wallsend, Whitley Bay and Blyth with a frequent service early to late every day.

The 306 starts out in the same direction but runs to Tynemouth from Newcastle. You can download a PDF file with all the latest times from the company websites, or the tourist information centres will send you paper copies. Even if you do not expect to use all the services, it's worth having the timetables for these buses, which link with the North Sea Trail, on your person in case of unforeseen circumstances.

There are also bus services to Ashington, which connect to Newcastle–Newbiggin services. ❶ www.arrivabus.co.uk/north-east

Arriva has an app (Arriva) which lets you buy your ticket and show it on your smartphone to the driver on entry.

Newbiggin is not yet on the X15 or X18 bus route so the only services are from Newcastle stopping also at Ashington Bus station:

X21 Newcastle bus station to Newbiggin The Woodhorn Museum can be accessed from this bus by leaving it at one of the bus stops in Woodhorn Road, inland of the Wansbeck Hospital, preferably where

the houses stop and allotments start, and making your way on foot to the A197, from which you can walk to the museum which is behind the woods on the far side.

North of Amble

Arriva bus no. X18 is the Northumbrian bus service

The X15 goes up and down the A1, more or less, and is a faster alternative for some journey/North Sea Trail access points. The two services are co-ordinated to some extent.

Just as the Coaster service provides an efficient back-up for walkers on southern section of this trail from Newcastle Gateshead to Whitley Bay, the Coast and Castles X18 Arriva bus provides a similar, if less frequent, service for all points north of Amble. Along with the X15 direct Newcastle–Berwick route along the A1, with which it often connects at main stopping points.

You could use this service as part of your strategy for tackling this northern section of the North Sea Trail as follows:

- Have a base somewhere along its route and plan a series of walks, which cover the ground from each base.

- Use it for unexpected events when you run out of time for any reason (there's so much to see, so little time).

- Avoid doing the bits that aren't great fun, and concentrate on the best bits (see introduction). Not allowed for sponsored walkers! They must face the complete challenge, rain or shine.

Useful Information

The only snag is that these buses finish running quite early at some points along the route, but with careful study and planning they can play a very useful part in covering the whole route.

Planning transport

Visit www.travelinescotland.com for a smartphone Traveline app which finds transport for you in Scotland on your smartphone or pad, and a VisitScotland Days Out app.

North of Berwick

Good regular bus services by Perrymans run between Burnmouth, Eyemouth, Coldingham and St Abbs.

Ask at Berwick-upon-Tweed TIC for timetables or go to:
ⓘ www.perrymansbuses.co.uk

The excellent website gives downloadable PDF timetables which you can print out or put on your smartphone and take with you. Of particular interest to Coast Path users will be the Berwick-upon-Tweed–Lindisfarne service.

The Perrymans timetable shows the connections from Newcastle to Beal, so that you can plan visits to Holy Island from any point south on the coast using this service in connection with the excellent Coast and Castles service.

The site also shows the services from Berwick-upon-Tweed to Burnside, Eyemouth, Coldingham and St Abbs giving you the choice to base yourself at any of these places whilst walking this southern Scottish section of the North Sea Trail, the Berwickshire Coast Path. You must visit Coldingham at some stage of your stay.

English free bus pass holders be warned, you have to pay on these buses once in Scotland!

Tourist information centres (TICs)

Newcastle

ⓘ www.newcastlegateshead.com

North Tyneside
(That's everywhere from Wallsend to St Mary's Lighthouse)
ⓘ www.northtyneside.gov.uk

This website covers all of its services so for accommodation click on 'Culture and Tourism', then 'Tourism' and then 'Where to stay' for a comprehensive list. It may be easier to google 'accommodation in North Tyneside' and click on 'Where to stay – North Tyneside Council' you will at least get directly to the tourist related info. The excellent 'Where to Stay' page is then hidden at the bottom of that page under 'Related documents', 'Accommodation in North Tyneside'.

There are quite a few listed B&Bs near the coast between Wallsend and Whitley Bay at a very good range of prices and standards from hostel-style to luxury.

North Tyneside's tourist information centres provide a wide range of information and services for residents and visitors alike including:

- Local and national tourist information
- Information on local attractions and events

- Information on accommodation in the area
- Book-a-bed-ahead service
- Bus, railway and public transport information
- Books and maps.

North Shields TIC
York Road, Whitley Bay, Tyne & Wear NE26 7SW
☎0191 643 5395
✉ ticwb@northtyneside.gov.uk
Monday–Saturday 9a.m.–5p.m.,

Whitley Bay TIC
Park Road, Whitley Bay, Tyne & Wear NE26 1EJ
☎0191 200 8535
✉ ticwb@northtyneside.gov.uk
Monday, Tuesday and Thursday–Saturday 9.30a.m.–5p.m. (closed for lunch 12.30p.m.–1.30p.m.), closed Wednesday and Sunday, open on Wednesday from 25th July–29th August 9.30a.m.–12.30p.m.

Northumberland

Morpeth TIC
The Chantry, Bridge Street, Morpeth Northumberland, NE61 1PD
☎01670 623455
Every day 9.30a.m.–5p.m. except bank holidays and Sundays in December when it will be open 11a.m.–4p.m.

Amble TIC
Queen Street, Amble, Northumberland NE65 0DQ
☎01665 712313
ℹ www.visitnorthumberland.com/amble
April–October daily including Sunday and bank holidays 10a.m.–5p.m., closed November–March

Craster TIC
Craster Car Park, Craster, Craster Northumberland NE66 3TW
☎01665 576007
ℹ www.visitnorthumberland.com/craster
April to October daily including Sunday and bank holidays 10a.m.–5p.m., during the winter it is only open on weekends and bank holidays 10.30a.m.–4p.m.

Seahouses TIC
Seafield Car Park, Seafield Road, Seahouses, Northumberland NE68 7SW
☎01670 625593 or ☎01665 720884
ℹ www.visitnorthumberland.com/seahouses
April–October daily including Sunday 10a.m.–5p.m., during the winter it is only open on weekends and bank holidays 11a.m.–3p.m.

Berwick TIC
106 Marygate, Berwick-upon-Tweed, Northumberland TD15 1BN
☎01670 622155
April–October Monday–Saturday 10a.m.–5p.m. open on Sunday 11a.m.–3p.m. only in June, July, August and September; November–March Monday–Saturday 10a.m.–4p.m.

The St Abbs Visitor Centre
Coldingham Road, St Abbs, Berwickshire TD14 5PL
✉ hello@stabbsvisitorcentre.co.uk
☎01890 771 672
April to October Monday–Sunday 10a.m.–5p.m.
Admission is free but donations are welcome, and vital to the success of the enterprise.

The St Abbs Visitor Centre is a registered independent Scottish charity providing a resource for both visitors and the local community.
ⓘ www.stabbsvisitorcentre.co.uk

The St Abbs Marine Station has an interesting website at
ⓘ www.marinestation.co.uk/stabbs
You can watch recent videos of the superb marine wildlife here. There are services for divers at the harbour.

St Abbs is a beautiful fishing village and immediately offshore is the St Abb's Head nature reserve. St Abb's Head is owned by the National Trust for Scotland and they have an information centre about the headland, with suggested walks and a host of fascinating historical information. The two information centres are free to visit. The National Trust centre is in a former barn next to its car park which is on a sharp bend in the road going into St Abbs. It's discreetly hidden away beneath trees at the bottom of the car park, which has a pedestrian way leading to it once you are out of the village.

The St Abbs Visitor Centre is in the old reading room high above the fishing harbour. There is a staircase going up to it from the harbour car park. It opened in the spring of 2011. The displays are quite different subjects from the National Trust centre. Both are really well presented and give a really good perspective on the area. You will get much more out of your visit if you have spent a bit of time in them before going on to walk St Abb's Head. There is a café in the village, in the old school, and another one at the harbour (licensed) and a shop.

The best time to visit if you are interested in birdwatching is from May–August, when kittiwakes, guillemots, razorbills, shags, and fulmars crowd onto the ledges. There's a telescope in the St Abbs Visitor Centre, which you can watch them through.

The termination of my recommended walk for those who have made it from Newcastle, is the historic St Abbs lighthouse and foghorn.

St Abb's Head National Nature Reserve Visitor Centre

1 April–31 October, daily 10a.m.–5p.m. Donations welcome (at the visitor centre).
☎ 0844 493 2256
The nature reserve is open at all times.

Belford

For Belford tourist information please visit www.visitnorthumberland.com/belford.

Lindisfarne Heritage Centre (not a TIC)
☎ 01289 389004

A particularly good explanation of the early mediaeval happenings on the island with implications for those who still think of these times as 'the Dark Ages', a period of ignorance and poverty that is supposed to have enveloped Europe following the collapse of the Roman Empire and lasted until the Renaissance.

Here you will find exhibitions covering most aspects of the history, wildlife and community of Lindisfarne through the centuries. An excellent local initiative. A good idea to visit before roaming the island if possible, and once again afterwards to answer all the queries you may have after visiting the place. You will find an impressive electronic version of the Lindisfarne Gospels and accompanying information showing the source of the materials used and countries throughout the known world. Entry fee, and very well worth it.

Museums in Tyne and Wear

🌐 www.twmuseums.org.uk

I recommend the Discovery Museum and the Laing Art Gallery in Newcastle, and the Great North Museum if you have more time.

The Woodhorn Museum between Ashington and Newbiggin (a 25-minute walk) has the most comprehensive exhibition in Northumberland of the coal-mining era (1894–1986). Some of the pit-top machinery has been preserved on its original site, and a series of realistic reconstructions of the pits, the cottage interiors, the miners' showers and lots of photos and paintings by the Pitmen Painters, show how life in these parts was in the last century. There is also a small collection of the mineworkers' colourful and distinctive banners.

I can thoroughly recommend the 25-minute walking detour from the coast path to Newbiggin-by-the-Sea. Look around the site and make sure you see the exhibition. If you visit the exhibition first, the rather forlorn

buildings will be easier to imagine in their heyday. There is a café on the site. Allow an hour or two for the visit in addition to getting there. (You can also walk from Ashington bus station.)

Open Wednesday–Sundays (but all week in school holidays including bank holidays); 18–19 February 2013, 1–2 and 8–9 April, 27–28 May and then every day from Monday 22 July up to and including Monday 2 September 2013. Opening hours April–September 10a.m.–5p.m. October–March 10a.m.–4p.m.

Entrance is free. Neither the express buses to Newbiggin nor the Coast and Castles buses stop there, so visitors have to walk or go by car. From the coast path at Newbiggin-by-the-Sea follow the pavement on the A197 to the main road and then the cycleway signed for Ashington into the Queen Elizabeth II Country Park. When I visited there were no signs to the museum within the Country Park, but it's in the south-east corner and you may catch sight of the winding gear through the woods at some point.

☎01670 624455
🌐 www.experiencewoodhorn.com/intro-to-woodhorn

Accommodation

I found vacant accommodation at all the locations, even in mid-summer and school holidays, booking ahead by checking online and sometimes ringing to arrange the next night. Sometimes there are special offers on the late booking sites. I had to go inland at a weekend once. Wiser individuals will work out their itinerary in advance and book ahead. Information online should enable you to do so or phone or email the various TICs.

Useful websites

Burnmouth
🌐 www.burnmouthcc.com

Coldingham
🌐 www.coldingham.info

Eyemouth activities
🌐 www.eyemouthharbour.org

Eyemouth Boating Tours
🌐 www.glassbottomboat.org

Lindisfarne
🌐 www.lindisfarne.org.uk

Newbiggin-by-the-Sea
🌐 www.newbigginbythesea.co.uk

Pease Bay
🌐 www.peasebay.co.uk

For tourist information:
🌐 www.scotborders.gov.uk

Walking Festival
🌐 www.borderswalking.com

Surfing – hire, instruction, sales
🌐 www.stvedas.co.uk

Diving
🌐 www.aquastars.co.uk/diving

For the Scottish Borders brochure
🌐 www.scotborders.gov.uk/downloads/file/430/berwickshire_coastal_path

Berwickshire Coastal Path runs from Berwick to Cockburnspath (ck is silent) 28 miles (45 km). The Berwickshire Coastal Path follows the second highest cliffs on the east coast of Britain. This rugged coastline is one of the most spectacular in Britain. This guide covers the route as far as St Abbs.

(To get to Edinburgh and the Forth Bridge you will have to follow the John Muir Way, see mention in Chapter 12.)

Useful addresses

English Heritage (North East)
Bessie Surtees House, 41-44 Sandhill, Newcastle NE1 3JF
☎ 0191 269 1200
✉ northeast@english-heritage.org.uk
🌐 www.english-heritage.org.uk

Long Distance Walkers Association
🌐 www.ldwa.org.uk

Join online for £13 and you will have access to loads of information about long-distance paths. Members can also download GPS and other maps for their smartphones/pads of the section from Cresswell to Berwick.

National Trust Coastal Properties Manager
8 St Aidans, Seahouses NE68 7SR
☎ 01665 720651

National Trust (North East)
Scots Gap, Morpeth, Northumberland
NE61 4EG
☎01670 774691
❶www.nationaltrust.org.uk

Natural England
North East Regional Office, The
Quadrant, Newburn Riverside,
Newcastle-upon-Tyne NE15 8NZ
☎0300 060 2219
❶www.naturalengland.org.uk

Lindisfarne National
Nature Reserve
Beal Station, Beal, Berwick-upon-Tweed
TD15 2SP
Holy Island tide timetable available
online
www.northumberland.gov.uk

Northumberland and
Tyneside Bird Club
3 Green Close, Whitley Bay
NE25 9SH
✉apusx@blueyonder.co.uk
☎0191 2522 744

Northumberland Coast AONB
County Hall, Morpeth NE61 2EF
☎01665 511203
✉tom.cadwallender@northumberland.
gov.uk
❶www.northumberlandcoastaonb.org

Northumberland Wildlife Trust
The Garden house, St Nicholas Park
Jubilee Road, Newcastle-upon-Tyne
NE3 3XT
☎01912 846 884
✉mail@northwt.org.uk
❶www.nwt.org.uk

Ramblers Association
Camelford House,
87-90 Albert Embankment,
London SE1 7TW
☎020 7359 8500
❶www.ramblers.org.uk

RSPB
1 Sirius House, Business Park,
Newcastle-upon-Tyne NE4 7YL
☎0191 233 4300
❶www.rspb.org.uk

Sustrans
❶www.sustrans.org.uk
Mainly known as a cycling organisation,
but many of their off-road routes also
provide wide walkways. The North Sea
Trail can be followed from Newcastle
to Cresswell, with the proviso that you
use the footways or public rights of way
advised in this guide for the very few
sections where there is no accompanying
footway. These are at East Sleekburn and
Lynemouth–Cresswell and instructions
are given to follow about 3 miles (4 km)
of roads with footways in each case.

YHA
Trevelyan House, Dimple Road, Matlock,
Derbyshire DE4 3YH
☎0870 870 8868
❶www.yha.org.uk
✉customerservices@yha.org.uk

Newbiggin Maritime Centre
Church Point, Newbiggin-by-the-Sea,
NE64 6DB
☎01670 819251
❶www.newbigginmaritimecentre.org.uk
This features a shop, café and exhibition.

The exhibition, which is worth a visit,
has a small charge, and is open all

year. You can also make donations to this locally run initiative. Morpeth TIC are probably the best people to contact for detailed tourist information and bookings for this area.

Smartphone and tablet maps

The Sustrans app for smartphones (free), National Cycle Network, shows all of the UK's Sustrans routes on an OS base. Search for the app 'the Complete National Cycle Network'. Before setting off, ensure you can store maps on your device without being connected to a network.

There are various electronic versions of OS maps, usually rather more out of date than the paper versions. They will be on your device all the time, so no connections are required once you have downloaded the right maps. They show limited parts of the cycle network with hollow green rings where the route is off-road. They do, however, show other legal rights of way, including the section of the Northumberland Coast Path, which lies within the AONB, from Cresswell to Berwick and most of the Berwickshire Coast Path. One such app is 'Outdoors GB and National Parks'. You have to buy the app and then maps for each region/county. That's three maps to cover most of this path (Tyne and Wear, Northumberland 1:25 000 and North East England 1:50 000). The 1:25 000 maps, as used in this book, will be best for walking this path.

With a GPS enabled smartphone you will at least know where you are, and with the maps in this book you will be able to stay on track even where signing and waymarking are absent.

Other places to visit near the Northumberland and Berwickshire coasts

Alnwick Castle and Castle Gardens which are outstanding. Specialist rose collection, good cafés, lively fountains. For reflections of the castle in the River Aln, follow the permissive path along the Aln.

Cragside National Trust Armstrong's house in the hills. First house in the world to be lit by electricity, lovely garden walks, lots of industrial archaeological interest.

Jarrow St Paul's Monastery (English Heritage) and Bede's World Museum

Newcastle Great North Museum

South Shields Arbeia Roman Fort and Museum

Bibliography

Anderson, Chrissie. *Walks on Holy Island* (Rural Arts, 2011).

Graham, Frank. *Holy Island a Short History and Guide* (Butler, 2005).

Holmes, Beryl. *Tales of the Border Reivers* (Northern Heritage, 2011).

Pevsner and Richmond. *Northumberland* (Penguin, 1957 et sequi).

Porter, Mark. *Coast and Castles* (Baytree Press, 2007).

Robson and Bradley. *Northumberland Coast Path* (Northumberland CC, 2011).

Rylance and Morrison. *A Visitor's Guide to Druridge Bay* (Belfry, 1989).

Scottish Borders Council. *Paths Around Eyemouth and the Berwickshire Coastal Path* (Scottish Borders Council, 2006).

Smith, Ian. *Northumbrian Coastline* (Sandhill Press, 1988).

Story, Joanna. *Lindisfarne Priory* (English Heritage, 2006).

Taylor, B. J., et al. *British Regional Geology, Northern England* (Fourth edition) (HMSO, 1971).

Trewin, N.K., ed. *The Geology of Scotland* (Geological Society, 2002).

Tristram, Kate. *The Story of Holy Island* (Canterbury Press, 2012).

Trueman, Sir Arthur, ed. *The Coalfields of Great Britain* (Edward Arnold, 1954).

Walker and Ward. *Fossil, Eyewitness Handbook* (Dorling Kindersley, 1992).

Warn, Christopher Robert. *Rocks and Scenery from Tyne to Tweed* (Frank Graham, 1975).

White, John Talbot. *The Scottish Border and Northumberland* (Eyre Methuen, 1978).

Woodcock, Nigel, and Strachan, Rob, eds. *Geological History of Britain and Ireland,* (Blackwell Science, 2000).

Young, Alan. *Suburban Railways of Tyneside* (Baistow, 1999).

The following booklets give comprehensive information on the following subjects relating to the northern section of the Northumberland Coast from Cresswell to Berwick (and St Abbs in the case of the marine-related topics).

Exploring the Plant life of the Northumberland AONB

Exploring the Shore in Northumberland and Berwickshire

Exploring the Buildings

Birdwatching

The Underwater World

Exploring the Geology and Landscape

Explore the Archaeology

The Official Guides to all of

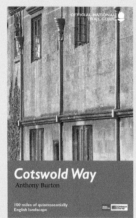

Cotswold Way
Anthony Burton

100 miles of quintessentially
English landscape

ISBN 978 1 84513 785 4

Cleveland Way
Ian Sampson

Over 100 miles of magnificent
walking on the North York Moors

ISBN 978 1 84513 781 6

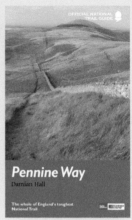

Pennine Way
Damian Hall

The whole of England's toughest
National Trail

ISBN 978 1 84513 718 2

Yorkshire Wolds Way
Roger Ratcliffe

A superbly tranquil walk through
the unspoilt chalk hills of Yorkshire

ISBN 978 178131 064 9

Pembrokeshire Coast Path
Wales Coast Path: St Dogmaels to Amroth
Brian John

ISBN 978 1 84513 782 3

South Downs Way
Paul Millmore

100 miles of glorious chalk downland
for the walker, cyclist and horse rider

ISBN 978 1 78131 088 5

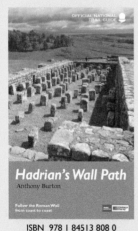

Hadrian's Wall Path
Anthony Burton

Follow the Roman Wall
from coast to coast

ISBN 978 1 84513 808 0

The Ridgeway
Anthony Burton

87 miles of downland walking
from Wiltshire to the Chilterns

ISBN 978 178131 063 2

North Downs Way
Colin Saunders

Follow the chalk ridge across South-East
England all the way to the sea

ISBN 978 178131 061 8